# Holt Psychology

## PRINCIPLES IN PRACTICE

**PORTFOLIO PROJECTS AND ASSESSMENT**

HOLT, RINEHART AND WINSTON
A Harcourt Education Company
Austin • Orlando • Chicago • New York • Toronto • London • San Diego

Cover: Sandra Dionisi/Stock Illustration Source



Printed in the United States of America

ISBN 0-03-068323-8

3 4 5 6 7 8 9 095 05 04

# CONTENTS

# PORTFOLIO PROJECTS AND ASSESSMENT

## *Introduction and Teaching Strategies*

The Portfolio Projects and Assessment material in this booklet is designed to provide teachers with an assessment tool other than testing. There are four pages of Assessment material for each chapter. The focus of this material matches a specific concept or concepts in the particular chapter.

The material for each chapter consists of the following sections:

- **PORTFOLIO: TEACHER'S NOTES** This page, designed for use by the teacher, consists of the following elements:

  *Background Information* provides a summary of the chapter content and describes the type of task the students will be doing.

  *Purpose* describes the students' purpose for performing the task.

  *Teaching Strategies* provides the teacher with several activities to introduce the task to the students, directives to assist students in completing the task, and often suggestions for ways to use the finished product.

  *Time Estimate* indicates an approximate amount of time students will need to complete the task.

- **PORTFOLIO: TASK SHEET** This page, to be used by students, describes the task the students will complete. This page consists of the following elements:

  *Introduction* provides students with a background of the concepts that their product should address.

  *Task* tells students what kind of product they are to produce.

  *Target Audience* provides students with the audience at which the product should be aimed.

  *Purpose* explains to students what they are to achieve by completing the product.

  *Procedure* provides students with specific steps for producing the product.

  *Assessment* refers students to the assessment form that will be used to evaluate the product.

- **PORTFOLIO: ASSESSMENT** This form is used to assess the product described in the Task Sheet. The Assessment form is used by both teachers and students. The form consists of a table that lists the criteria used in the assessment of the product. Each item in the list is to be evaluated according to a performance level of excellent (3), average (2), or unsatisfactory (1).

  By referring to the form while working on their product, students gain an awareness of the standards by which they will be evaluated. After completing the product, students are directed to use the form to assess their final product. Each Assessment form gives directions for computing the final score for the product. It also provides space for students to suggest ways in which the product might be improved.

- **BUILDING YOUR PORTFOLIO CHECKLIST** This form consists of directives and a Checklist for students to use as they build their portfolios. The Checklist, provided for each chapter, supplies students with specific steps they should follow in completing the relevant portion of the particular project. Students should use the blank line that precedes each step to check off the step as it is completed.

CHAPTER

# 1



# WHAT IS PSYCHOLOGY?

## *Exploring the Field of Psychology*

**BACKGROUND INFORMATION** Chapter 1 presents students with information about the field of psychology. Students are given an overview of what psychology is and the kinds of work that psychologists do. The chapter also traces the development of the field of psychology and current perspectives in psychology. In this assessment activity, students are asked to use this information to create a pamphlet to help other students examine the possibilities of a career in psychology.

**PURPOSE** To create a pamphlet that presents information about the work of psychologists, the various areas of specialization available for a career in psychology, and the personal traits that might be necessary to pursue a career in each area of psychology.

**TEACHING STRATEGIES** Before students begin work on the pamphlet, discuss with them the factors involved in deciding on a career. List the factors on the board, and have students choose the three factors they think are most important.

Before students begin the assignment, have them examine the Pamphlet Assessment form on page 3 to review the standards by which they will be evaluated.

Before students work on the pamphlet section that suggests characteristics that might be necessary to pursue a career in psychology, have students work in small groups to brainstorm personal characteristics that they think might be important. Students may want to use a question checklist for this part of the pamphlet, asking such questions as: Do you try to figure out why people behave as they do?

Stress to students the importance of making the pamphlet interesting and attractive—something a person will want to pick up and read. Encourage them to be creative in the way they present the information in their pamphlets.

After students have completed their pamphlets, have them evaluate their work by using the Pamphlet Assessment form on page 3. Use the same form for your evaluation of the work.

Display completed pamphlets for students in your school to use.

**TIME ESTIMATE** Approximately 7 50-minute class sessions, or about 6 hours.

Name ______________________ Date ____________ Class ____________

CHAPTER 1

PORTFOLIO: TASK SHEET

# WHAT IS PSYCHOLOGY?

## *Exploring the Field of Psychology*

### INTRODUCTION

Many high school students are thinking of what they will do with their lives. Choosing a career that is right for them is one of the most important decisions they will have to make. A possible career might be one in the field of psychology. However, how will they know whether this field would be right for them?

**TASK** Create a pamphlet that will serve as a guidebook to students interested in pursuing a career in psychology.

**TARGET AUDIENCE** Your pamphlet should target juniors and seniors in your school who are exploring various careers.

**PURPOSE** The purpose of the pamphlet is to give your target audience an overview of the work of psychologists. The pamphlet will explain the goals of psychology and the various specialization areas of psychology in which students might be interested in working. The pamphlet should also suggest questions that students might ask themselves to decide whether a career in psychology is one that interests them.

### PROCEDURE

1. Create sections in your pamphlet that address the following topics: the goals of psychology, the various kinds of work that psychologists do, and the personal characteristics that might be necessary to pursue a career in psychology.

2. Decide on the kinds of visuals that you will use in your pamphlet.

3. Make a rough draft of your pamphlet. Decide how many pages you will have, and outline the basic information that will appear on each page.

4. Write the text that will appear on each page. Be sure that each section includes an interesting heading. Make sure that the text and visuals combine to make the information clear.

5. Edit the first draft of your text.

6. Rewrite the draft, and use the Pamphlet Assessment form to identify improvements that you should make.

7. Make a final copy of your pamphlet, and present it to your teacher.

### ASSESSMENT

Use the Pamphlet Assessment form to evaluate your pamphlet.

Name ______________________ Date ____________ Class ____________

CHAPTER 1

PORTFOLIO: ASSESSMENT

# WHAT IS PSYCHOLOGY?

## *Pamphlet Assessment*

This form is designed to help you evaluate your pamphlet. Your teacher will use the same form to evaluate your work. Read the criteria listed. Then circle the number to the right of each criterion that most closely reflects your personal evaluation of your pamphlet.

| | Performance Levels | | |
|---|---|---|---|
| **Criteria** | **Excellent** | **Average** | **Unsatisfactory** |
| 1. The purpose of the pamphlet is clear. | 3 | 2 | 1 |
| 2. The pamphlet is well organized. | 3 | 2 | 1 |
| 3. The pamphlet demonstrates knowledge of the purpose of the assignment. | 3 | 2 | 1 |
| 4. The visuals in the pamphlet help clarify the information in the pamphlet. | 3 | 2 | 1 |
| 5. The visuals in the pamphlet are creative and add to the overall look of the pamphlet. | 3 | 2 | 1 |
| 6. The pamphlet is neat and legible. | 3 | 2 | 1 |
| 7. The pamphlet is understandable and interesting. | 3 | 2 | 1 |
| 8. The pamphlet reflects correct spelling, punctuation, and grammar. | 3 | 2 | 1 |
| 9. The pamphlet includes all the required elements. | 3 | 2 | 1 |
| 10. The pamphlet communicates well to the target audience. | 3 | 2 | 1 |

To compute the score for your pamphlet, add the numbers you have circled and divide the result by 10.

▶ **Total score for pamphlet** ____________

The pamphlet can be improved by ______________________

______________________

______________________

Name ______________________________ Date ______________ Class ______________

CHAPTER 1

BUILDING YOUR PORTFOLIO CHECKLIST

# WHAT IS PSYCHOLOGY?

## *Building Your Portfolio*

**STEP 1 (CHAPTER 1)**

Select a specific area of psychology that interests you. For that specific area, formulate a research question from your daily experience.

How does your research question relate to the specialized area of psychology you selected? What other areas could possibly benefit from your findings? Write your answers to these questions in the form of a paragraph to be used as an introduction to an oral report. Show the paragraph to your teacher. Use the following checklist.

______ State the specific area of psychology that interests you.

______ Decide on a research question.

______ Explain how your research question relates to the specialized area of psychology you selected.

______ Decide whether other areas of psychology might benefit from the answer to your research question.

______ Explain how other areas of psychology might benefit from the answer to your research question.

______ Write a paragraph explaining how your research question relates to the specialized area of psychology you selected.

______ Teacher's initials

CHAPTER

# 2 PSYCHOLOGICAL METHODS

PORTFOLIO: TEACHER'S NOTES

## *Conducting Scientific Research*

**BACKGROUND INFORMATION** Chapter 2 presents students with information about the procedures and steps psychologists follow in conducting scientific research. Students are given an overview of the various methods psychologists and other scientists use to answer research questions or to test hypotheses. In this assessment activity, students are asked to use this information to conduct research and write a research report that shows what they have learned about the procedures involved in conducting psychological research.

**PURPOSE** To write a research report that explains the procedures involved in conducting scientific research—forming a research question, forming a hypothesis, testing the hypothesis, analyzing the results, and drawing conclusions.

**TEACHING STRATEGIES** Before students begin work on the research report, discuss with them the procedures involved in conducting research. Write these on the board in outline form. Point out to students that they should follow this outline when writing their report. Then have students list the various methods used to answer research questions and to test hypotheses. Ask students to explain which method they would use to test the following hypotheses: (1) Adults listen to the radio more than teens do. (2) People always cross their legs when they are sitting. (3) Dogs that are taken for long walks sleep longer than dogs that are never taken for walks.

Before students begin the assignment, have them examine the Research Report Assessment form on page 7. Be sure they understand the standards by which they will be evaluated.

Encourage students to choose a research question and a hypothesis that can be tested within three to four hours.

Before students begin step 3 under Procedure, have them work in small groups to discuss which research method would best test the hypothesis.

After students have completed their research reports, have them evaluate their work by using the Research Report Assessment form on page 7. Use the same form for your evaluation of the work.

Make the completed research reports available to the class.

**TIME ESTIMATE** Approximately 8 50-minute class sessions, or about 6 to 7 hours.

CHAPTER 2

PORTFOLIO: TASK SHEET

# PSYCHOLOGICAL METHODS

## *Conducting Scientific Research*

### INTRODUCTION

Psychology is the study of behavior and mental processes. Psychologists learn about these processes by conducting scientific research. They use a variety of psychological methods to test their research questions and hypotheses. They analyze their results and draw conclusions. All the information scientists gather is written in the form of a research report so that others can learn about the results of the research study.

**TASK** Write a research report that shows the steps that psychologists follow in conducting scientific research.

**TARGET AUDIENCE** Your research report should target juniors and seniors in your school who are interested in conducting or interpreting scientific research.

**PURPOSE** The purpose of the research report is to provide your target audience with an overview of the steps that psychologists follow when they conduct scientific research. The research report will record the findings of a study by following the steps used in scientific research.

### PROCEDURE

1. Formulate a research question from daily experience, psychological theory, folklore, or common knowledge. Record your research question.
2. Formulate a hypothesis about the answer to the research question.
3. Test your hypothesis using one of the research methods psychologists use: survey, case study, observation, or experiment. Record the type of research method used, explain the procedures of the method, and describe the results obtained.
4. Analyze your results. Record your interpretation of the results.
5. Draw conclusions about your research question and your hypothesis. Write a summary that explains your conclusions.
6. Decide on the kinds of graphics (if applicable) you will use to present your results.
7. Make a rough draft of your research report.
8. Edit the rough draft of your report.
9. Rewrite the draft, and use the Research Report Assessment form to identify improvements that you should make.
10. Make a final copy of your research report, and present it to your teacher.

### ASSESSMENT

Use the Research Report Assessment form to evaluate your research report.

Name ______________________ Date ____________ Class ____________

CHAPTER 2

PORTFOLIO: ASSESSMENT

# PSYCHOLOGICAL METHODS

## *Research Report Assessment*

This form is designed to help you evaluate your research report. Your teacher will use the same form to evaluate your work. Read the criteria listed. Then circle the number to the right of each criterion that most closely reflects your personal evaluation of your research report.

| Criteria | Performance Levels Excellent | Average | Unsatisfactory |
|---|---|---|---|
| 1. The purpose of the research report is clear. | 3 | 2 | 1 |
| 2. The research report is well organized into paragraphs with clear main ideas and appropriate supporting details. | 3 | 2 | 1 |
| 3. The conclusion summarizes the main points of the report and indicates that the hypothesis has been proved or disproved. | 3 | 2 | 1 |
| 4. The research report demonstrates that the purpose of the assignment is understood. | 3 | 2 | 1 |
| 5. The research report uses the student's own ideas. | 3 | 2 | 1 |
| 6. Appropriate sources (if applicable) are included in the research report. | 3 | 2 | 1 |
| 7. The graphics (if applicable) add to the clarity of information in the research report. | 3 | 2 | 1 |
| 8. The research report is formatted according to directions. | 3 | 2 | 1 |
| 9. The research report reflects correct spelling, grammar, and punctuation. | 3 | 2 | 1 |
| 10. The research report is neat and legible. | 3 | 2 | 1 |

To compute the score for your research report, add the numbers you have circled and divide the result by 10.

▶ **Total score for research report** ____________

The research report can be improved by ______________________________

______________________________________________

______________________________________________

Name ______________________________ Date ______________ Class ______________

CHAPTER 2

BUILDING YOUR PORTFOLIO CHECKLIST

# PSYCHOLOGICAL METHODS

## *Building Your Portfolio*

**USING RESEARCH TECHNIQUES**

Formulate a hypothesis about a type of behavior that interests you. For example, you might want to study the television viewing habits of adults or the ways in which your classmates spend their free time. Then test your hypothesis.

**STEP 2 (CHAPTER 2)**

How did you test your hypothesis? What do you believe your findings or observations indicate? Did you collect enough data to display your results accurately and completely? What conclusions can you draw from your findings? If your findings or observations did not support your hypothesis, how should you change your theory or hypothesis?

Create written and visual materials to analyze your research method and results. Make a rough draft of your written and visual materials, and show it to your teacher. Use the following checklist.

_______ State your hypothesis.

_______ Explain, in detail, the method you chose for testing your hypothesis and the steps you followed.

_______ Explain what you believe your findings or observations indicate.

_______ Decide whether you collected enough data to analyze your results accurately and completely.

_______ Describe the conclusions that you can draw from your findings.

_______ Determine whether your findings or observations support your hypothesis, and change your theory or hypothesis if necessary.

_______ Create a rough draft of the written and visual materials to be used in the oral report.

_______ Teacher's initials

CHAPTER 3



# BIOLOGY AND BEHAVIOR

## *Learning About Behavior*

**BACKGROUND INFORMATION** Chapter 3 presents students with information about the work of biological psychologists. Students learn that biological psychologists study ways in which the brain, the nervous system, the endocrine system, and heredity affect human behavior, thought, and emotions. In this assessment activity, students are asked to use this information to create a poster to help them identify ways in which biology affects behavior.

**PURPOSE** To create a poster that gives examples of ways in which people's behavior is affected by the nervous system, the brain, the endocrine system, and heredity.

**TEACHING STRATEGIES** Before students begin work on the poster, review with them the functions of the nervous system, the brain, and the endocrine system. Then ask students to explain the role of chromosomes and genes in heredity.

Before students begin the assignment, have them examine the Poster Assessment form on page 11. Be sure they understand the standards by which they will be evaluated.

Before students work on the poster, have them meet in small groups to brainstorm ideas to illustrate the ways in which the nervous system, the brain, the endocrine system, and heredity affect behavior.

After students have completed their posters, have them evaluate their work by using the Poster Assessment form on page 11. Use the same form for your evaluation of the work.

Display the completed posters in the classroom.

**TIME ESTIMATE** Approximately 2 50-minute class sessions, or about 1 1/2 to 2 hours.

Name ______________________ Date __________ Class __________

CHAPTER 3

PORTFOLIO: TASK SHEET

# BIOLOGY AND BEHAVIOR

## *Learning About Behavior*

### INTRODUCTION

Biological psychologists study the ways in which people's behavior and psychological processes are linked to biological structures and processes. Biological psychologists study the ways in which the nervous system, the brain, the endocrine system, and heredity affect both biological and psychological processes. How do these biological factors affect behavior?

**TASK** Create a poster to illustrate the ways in which the nervous system, the brain, the endocrine system, and heredity affect behavior in adolescents.

**TARGET AUDIENCE** Your poster should target adolescents who are interested in learning about biological causes of their behavior, thoughts, and emotions.

**PURPOSE** The purpose of the poster is to provide your target audience with an overview of biological and hereditary factors that affect behavior. The poster will include examples of the ways in which the nervous system, the brain, the endocrine system, and heredity affect behavior in adolescents.

### PROCEDURE

1. Create four sections on your poster to illustrate the following influences on behavior: the nervous system, the brain, the endocrine system, and heredity.
2. Decide on the kinds of visuals you will use in your poster.
3. Make a rough draft of your poster. Sketch out the basic information and visuals that will appear in each section of your poster.
4. Write a rough draft of the text that will appear in each section. Be sure to include an interesting heading for each section of your poster. Make sure that your text and visuals combine to make the information on the poster clear.
5. Edit the first draft of your text.
6. Rewrite the draft, and use the Poster Assessment form to identify improvements that you should make.
7. Make a final copy of your poster, and present it to your teacher.

### ASSESSMENT

Use the Poster Assessment form to evaluate your poster.

Name ______________________ Date ____________ Class ____________

CHAPTER 3

PORTFOLIO: ASSESSMENT

# BIOLOGY AND BEHAVIOR

## *Poster Assessment*

This form is designed to help you evaluate your poster. Your teacher will use the same form to evaluate your work. Read the criteria listed. Then circle the number to the right of each criterion that most closely reflects your personal evaluation of your poster.

| Criteria | Performance Levels<br>Excellent | <br>Average | <br>Unsatisfactory |
|---|---|---|---|
| 1. The purpose of the poster is clear. | 3 | 2 | 1 |
| 2. The poster presents clear main ideas with connecting details to give the poster a sense of wholeness. | 3 | 2 | 1 |
| 3. The information in the poster is accurate. | 3 | 2 | 1 |
| 4. The poster demonstrates that the purpose of the assignment is understood. | 3 | 2 | 1 |
| 5. The design elements—space, shape, color, and texture—add to the overall look of the poster. | 3 | 2 | 1 |
| 6. The visuals on the poster are creative, add to the overall look of the poster, and clarify the information on the poster. | 3 | 2 | 1 |
| 7. The poster is attractive and holds the viewer's interest. | 3 | 2 | 1 |
| 8. The poster reflects correct spelling, grammar, and punctuation. | 3 | 2 | 1 |
| 9. The poster communicates well to the target audience. | 3 | 2 | 1 |

To compute the score for your poster, add the numbers you have circled and divide the result by 9.

▶ Total score for poster____________

The poster can be improved by ______________________________

______________________________

______________________________

Name ______________________ Date __________ Class __________

CHAPTER 3

BUILDING YOUR PORTFOLIO CHECKLIST

# BIOLOGY AND BEHAVIOR

## *Building Your Portfolio*

### THE BODY POLITIC

You may have heard the term *body politic,* which refers to a group of people organized into a collective unit such as a nation. Now that you have read about the makeup of the human body and mind, evaluate the extent to which they are similar to an entire nation such as the United States.

### STEP 1 (CHAPTER 3)

What is the "biology" of the United States? Does the United States have "neurons," and if so, what are they? Does the nation have a nervous system? A brain? What about an endocrine system? What aspects of the United States might be considered a result of heredity, and what aspects might be due to "nurture"?

Create two graphic organizers that, side by side, compare the makeup of the human body with that of the United States. One will show the biological components of the human body and brain; the other will show the social, political, and/or economic components of the United States. Make rough drafts of the graphic organizers, and show them to your teacher. Use the following checklist.

______ Determine what the "biology" of the United States is.

______ Decide what the "neurons" of the United States are.

______ Determine what the "nervous system" of the United States is.

______ Determine what the "endocrine system" of the United States is.

______ Decide which aspects of the United States are a result of "heredity."

______ Decide which aspects of the United States are due to "nurture."

______ Make a rough draft of the graphic organizer showing biological components of the human body.

______ Make a rough draft of the graphic organizer showing social, political, and economic components of the United States.

______ Arrange the graphic organizers so that they compare the components of the human body with the components of the United States.

______ Teacher's initials

CHAPTER 4

PORTFOLIO: TEACHER'S NOTES

# SENSATION AND PERCEPTION

## *Demonstrating Sensory Perception*

**BACKGROUND INFORMATION** Chapter 4 presents information about sensory impressions (sensation) and the way in which the brain makes sense of or interprets these impressions (perception). Students are given an overview of the ways that the various senses work and how to distinguish between sensation and perception. In this assessment activity, students are asked to use this information to create and conduct a demonstration to help them understand how people organize and interpret their environment through sensation and perception.

**PURPOSE** To create a demonstration that illustrates one of the ways in which people understand and organize their environment through sensation and perception.

**TEACHING STRATEGIES** Before students begin work on the demonstration, review with them the examples of sensory perception shown in the following figures in the text chapter: Figures 4.5, 4.6, and 4.11 through 4.18. Discuss with students how each figure illustrates a different sensory perception. Ask students to discuss how the examples shown in the figures help explain the concept being taught.

Before students begin the assignment, have them examine the Demonstration Assessment form on page 15 to review the standards by which they will be evaluated.

Encourage students to choose a demonstration that can be presented within 5 to 10 minutes or less.

Review each student's demonstration idea before the demonstrations are tested. Analyze demonstration ideas for length, content, and safety.

Allow students time to test their demonstration on fellow students.

Arrange a time and a place where students can present their demonstrations in a type of psychology or science fair.

After students have completed their demonstrations, have them evaluate their work by using the Demonstration Assessment form on page 15. Use the same form for your evaluation of the work.

**TIME ESTIMATE** Approximately 3 50-minute class sessions, or about 2 1/2 hours.

Name ______________________ Date ____________ Class ____________

CHAPTER 4

PORTFOLIO: TASK SHEET

# SENSATION AND PERCEPTION

## *Demonstrating Sensory Perception*

**INTRODUCTION**

It is important to know the difference between sensation and perception and to know how each adds to an understanding of the world around you. You experience the world through your senses and by the way you interpret, or perceive, the information your senses absorb. Certain laws can be applied to the different ways in which people make sense of sensory information. Psychologists use demonstrations to help explain the laws of sensory perception.

**TASK** Create a demonstration that will explain a law of sensory perception.

**TARGET AUDIENCE** Your demonstration should target first- and second-year students in your school who have not studied the laws of sensory perception.

**PURPOSE** The purpose of the demonstration is to provide your target audience with an illustration that helps explain a law of sensory perception. The demonstration will help explain how sensation and perception contribute to an understanding of our environment.

**PROCEDURE**

1. Choose a law of sensory perception that you wish to demonstrate.
2. Create a way to demonstrate the sensory perception. Your demonstration should conclude with an explanation or summary of the sensory perception law demonstrated.
3. Decide on the kinds of graphics and/or other materials you will use in your demonstration.
4. Test your demonstration on fellow classmates to make sure that the sensory perception you wish to demonstrate is illustrated properly.
5. Analyze your demonstration and the reaction of the classmates who saw it.
6. Revise your demonstration on the basis of your analysis.
7. Present your demonstration to your target audience.

**ASSESSMENT**

Use the Demonstration Assessment form to evaluate your demonstration.

Name ______________________ Date ____________ Class ____________

CHAPTER 4

PORTFOLIO: ASSESSMENT

# SENSATION AND PERCEPTION

## *Demonstration Assessment*

This form is designed to help you evaluate your demonstration. Your teacher will use the same form to evaluate your work. Read the criteria listed. Then circle the number to the right of each criterion that most closely reflects your personal evaluation of your demonstration.

| Criteria | Performance Levels<br>Excellent | <br>Average | <br>Unsatisfactory |
|---|---|---|---|
| 1. The purpose of the demonstration is clear. | 3 | 2 | 1 |
| 2. The demonstration is well organized and supports the purpose. | 3 | 2 | 1 |
| 3. The information in the demonstration is accurate and conveys the most important points relating to the purpose. | 3 | 2 | 1 |
| 4. The demonstration reflects knowledge of the purpose of the assignment. | 3 | 2 | 1 |
| 5. The graphics and/or other materials used in the demonstration add to the clarity of the demonstration. | 3 | 2 | 1 |
| 6. The demonstrator(s) can be seen and heard (when appropriate). | 3 | 2 | 1 |
| 7. The demonstration is understandable and holds the audience's attention. | 3 | 2 | 1 |

To compute the score for your demonstration, add the numbers you have circled and divide the result by 7.

▶ **Total score for demonstration** ____________

The demonstration can be improved by ______________________________

______________________________________________

______________________________________________

Name ______________________________ Date ______________ Class ______________

CHAPTER 4

BUILDING YOUR PORTFOLIO CHECKLIST

# SENSATION AND PERCEPTION

## *Building Your Portfolio*

**STEP 2 (CHAPTER 4)**

How does the United States sense and perceive information? Does it have equivalents to the senses of vision, hearing, smell, and taste? Does it have skin senses and body senses? Once the nation takes in information, how does it process that information? What principles of perceptual organization does it use? To what extent is it susceptible to perceptual illusions?

Create a chart that compares humans and the nation in terms of sensation and perception. Make a rough draft of the chart, and show it to your teacher. Use the following checklist.

______ Determine how the United States senses and perceives information.

______ Decide whether or not the United States has equivalents to the senses of vision, hearing, smell, and taste.

______ Determine whether the United States has skin senses and body senses.

______ Explain how the United States processes information.

______ Explain the principles of perceptual organization that the United States uses.

______ Determine to what extent the United States is subject to illusions.

______ Make a rough draft of a chart comparing humans and the United States in terms of sensation and perception.

______ Teacher's initials

CHAPTER

# 5



# CONSCIOUSNESS

## *Analyzing Consciousness*

**BACKGROUND INFORMATION** Chapter 5 discusses the nature of consciousness. Students are given an overview of the factors that affect consciousness, such as wakefulness, altered states, and drugs. In this assessment activity, students are asked to use this information to create a public-service radio announcement about the effects of drugs on consciousness.

**PURPOSE** To create a public-service radio announcement that explains how drug use affects consciousness.

**TEACHING STRATEGIES** Before students begin work on the public-service radio announcement, discuss with them the kinds of public-service announcements they have heard on the radio, seen and heard on television, and read in newspapers and magazines. Discuss the purpose, the content, and the effectiveness of such announcements.

Before students begin the assignment, have them examine the Public-Service Radio Announcement Assessment form on page 19 to review the standards by which they will be evaluated.

Tell students that their public-service announcements should last between 30 seconds and 1 minute.

Allow students time to practice their public-service radio announcements.

Arrange to have students deliver their public-service radio announcements on the public address system at school. Perhaps one per day or one per week could be read to the student body during morning or homeroom announcements.

After students have completed their public-service radio announcements, have them evaluate their work by using the Public-Service Radio Announcement Assessment form on page 19. Use the same form for your evaluation of the work.

**TIME ESTIMATE** Approximately 2 50-minute class sessions, or about 1 1/2 to 2 hours.

Name ______________________________ Date ______________ Class ______________

CHAPTER 5

PORTFOLIO: TASK SHEET

# CONSCIOUSNESS

## *Analyzing Consciousness*

**INTRODUCTION**
Consciousness can be affected by drugs. A person's perceptions, emotions, and moods can be changed by drugs. Depressants, stimulants, and hallucinogens are types of drugs that can distort consciousness. Psychologists have studied the effect of drugs on people's consciousness. Knowing how drugs can affect a person's consciousness may help people avoid the use of nonprescribed drugs.

**TASK** Create a public-service radio announcement that explains the effects of a drug on a person's consciousness.

**TARGET AUDIENCE** Your public-service radio announcement should target students in your school.

**PURPOSE** The purpose of the public-service radio announcement is to provide your target audience with an explanation of the effects of a drug on a person's consciousness.

**PROCEDURE**

1. Choose a drug issue to address.
2. Make an outline of the points you want to cover in your public-service radio announcement.
3. Make a rough draft of the script for your public-service radio announcement.
4. Edit the first draft of your script.
5. Choose music and/or other audio effects to help convey your message.
6. Read the draft of your script to a partner. Ask your partner for comments on the content, the music and/or other audio effects, and the delivery of your public-service radio announcement.
7. Revise your public-service radio announcement.
8. Present your public-service radio announcement to your target audience.

**ASSESSMENT**
Use the Public-Service Radio Announcement Assessment form to evaluate your announcement.

Name ______________________ Date ____________ Class ____________

CHAPTER 5

PORTFOLIO: ASSESSMENT

# CONSCIOUSNESS

## *Public-Service Radio Announcement Assessment*

This form is designed to help you evaluate your public-service radio announcement. Your teacher will use the same form to evaluate your work. Read the criteria listed. Then circle the number to the right of each criterion that most closely reflects your personal evaluation of your public-service radio announcement.

| | Performance Levels | | |
|---|---|---|---|
| **Criteria** | **Excellent** | **Average** | **Unsatisfactory** |
| 1. The topic and purpose of the public-service radio announcement are clear. | 3 | 2 | 1 |
| 2. The script is appropriate for the target audience. | 3 | 2 | 1 |
| 3. The public-service radio announcement is organized and focused on its purpose. | 3 | 2 | 1 |
| 4. The information in the public-service radio announcement is accurate and conveys the most important points of its message. | 3 | 2 | 1 |
| 5. The music and/or other sound effects add to the clarity and effectiveness of the public-service radio announcement. | 3 | 2 | 1 |
| 6. The dialogue is interesting and enhances the effectiveness of the announcement. | 3 | 2 | 1 |
| 7. The public-service radio announcement demonstrates knowledge of the purpose of the assignment. | 3 | 2 | 1 |
| 8. The public-service radio announcement holds the audience's attention and communicates the intended message to the audience. | 3 | 2 | 1 |

To compute the score for your public-service radio announcement, add the numbers you have circled and divide the result by 8.

▶ **Total score for public-service radio announcement** ____________

The public-service radio announcement can be improved by ____________

______________________________________________

Name ______________________ Date ____________ Class ____________

CHAPTER 5

BUILDING YOUR PORTFOLIO CHECKLIST

# CONSCIOUSNESS

## *Building Your Portfolio*

**STEP 3 (CHAPTER 5)**

To what extent does the United States have consciousness similar to that of individual people? What are the different ways in which the nation is conscious? Does the nation ever experience "altered states of consciousness," and if so, what are they? How are they caused?

Write an essay comparing and contrasting people's consciousness with the nation's consciousness. Create a rough draft of the essay, and show it to your teacher. Organize all the written and visual materials from this chapter and from Chapters 3 and 4 to be used in your oral report analyzing similarities and differences between the human body and the United States. Use the following checklist.

______ Determine to what extent the United States has a consciousness similar to that of people.

______ Describe the different ways in which the United States is conscious.

______ Determine whether the United States ever experiences "altered states of consciousness," and if so, explain what they are.

______ Explain what might cause such "altered states of consciousness."

______ Create a rough draft of an essay comparing and contrasting individuals' consciousness with national consciousness.

______ Organize your written and visual materials (from Chapters 3, 4, and 5) to be used in your oral report analyzing similarities and differences between the human body and the United States.

______ Teacher's initials

CHAPTER



# 6 LEARNING

## *Understanding Learning*

**BACKGROUND INFORMATION** Chapter 6 presents students with information about the principles of learning. The chapter describes some of the processes through which people and animals learn. Students are given an overview of the several types of learning and the processes involved in each type. In this assessment activity, students are asked to use this information to give an oral presentation explaining a type of learning and the processes involved in it.

**PURPOSE** To give an oral presentation that explains a type of learning and the processes involved in it.

**TEACHING STRATEGIES** Before students begin work on the oral presentation, ask them to summarize the examples given in the chapter to explain and describe classical conditioning, operant conditioning, cognitive factors in learning, and the PQ4R method of learning. Discuss with students how the examples helped them understand and remember important concepts about learning.

Before students begin the assignment, have them examine the Oral Presentation Without Visual Aids Assessment form on page 23 to review the standards by which they will be evaluated.

Allow time for students to practice their oral presentations with a partner before sharing them with the class.

After students have completed their oral presentations, have them evaluate their work by using the Oral Presentation Without Visual Aids Assessment form on page 23. Use the same form for your evaluation of the work.

**TIME ESTIMATE** Approximately 2 50-minute class sessions, or about 1 1/2 to 2 hours.

Name ______________________ Date ____________ Class ____________

CHAPTER 6

PORTFOLIO: TASK SHEET

# LEARNING

## *Understanding Learning*

**INTRODUCTION**
There are several types of learning and several processes involved in each type of learning. Knowing and understanding the key concepts of the various types of learning can help you become a better learner. One way to help yourself understand and remember these concepts is to think about some skills you learned or about some knowledge you gained. If you cannot think of personal experiences, try to think of the experiences of others whose behavior provides examples of the kinds of learning processes described.

**TASK** Give an oral presentation without visual aids that uses personal experiences or experiences of others to explain a type of learning and the processes involved in it.

**TARGET AUDIENCE** Your oral presentation without visual aids should target your classmates.

**PURPOSE** The purpose of the oral presentation without visual aids is to provide your target audience with examples of a type of learning and the processes involved in it in order to help your classmates understand and remember the concepts of learning.

**PROCEDURE**

1. Choose a type of learning and the processes involved in it to serve as the topic of your oral presentation without visual aids.
2. Decide on the examples, from your personal experiences or from the experiences of others you know, to include in your oral presentation. The examples will help explain the type of learning you chose for your oral presentation without visual aids.
3. Make an outline for your oral presentation.
4. Create a rough draft of your oral presentation. Be sure to include an opening statement that explains the purpose of your oral presentation, a body of information that provides details and examples of experiences, and a summary that ties the information together.
5. Edit the first draft of your oral presentation.
6. Practice the oral presentation in front of a video camera or in front of a mirror. Watch your presentation. Make appropriate adjustments in your delivery. Listen to your presentation.
7. Rework the draft of your oral presentation to make sure that the words flow smoothly. Use the Oral Presentation Without Visual Aids Assessment form to identify improvements that you can make.
8. Using index cards, write short notes that will help you remember what you want to say in your oral presentation.
9. Practice your oral presentation using the note cards.
10. Deliver your oral presentation to your target audience.

**ASSESSMENT**
Use the Oral Presentation Without Video Aids Assessment form to evaluate your oral presentation.

Name ______________________________ Date ______________ Class ______________

CHAPTER 6

PORTFOLIO: ASSESSMENT

# LEARNING

## *Oral Presentation Without Visual Aids Assessment*

This form is designed to help you evaluate your oral presentation without visual aids. Your teacher will use the same form to evaluate your work. Read the criteria listed. Then circle the number to the right of each criterion that most closely reflects your personal evaluation of your oral presentation without visual aids.

| | Performance Levels | | |
|---|---|---|---|
| **Criteria** | **Excellent** | **Average** | **Unsatisfactory** |
| 1. The purpose of the oral presentation is clear. | 3 | 2 | 1 |
| 2. The oral presentation is well organized and easy to follow. | 3 | 2 | 1 |
| 3. The information in the oral presentation is accurate and relevant to the purpose. The details and examples presented make the main ideas meaningful to the audience. | 3 | 2 | 1 |
| 4. The presenter speaks fluently without having to constantly read from notes. | 3 | 2 | 1 |
| 5. The presenter makes eye contact with the audience. | 3 | 2 | 1 |
| 6. The oral presentation is interesting and holds the attention of the audience. | 3 | 2 | 1 |
| 7. The presenter appears confident and shows interest and enthusiasm. | 3 | 2 | 1 |
| 8. The presenter ties the information together with a closing summary. | 3 | 2 | 1 |

To compute the score for your oral presentation without visual aids, add the numbers you have circled and divide the result by 8.

▶ **Total score for oral presentation without visual aids** ______________

The oral presentation without visual aids can be improved by ____________________

____________________________________________________________

____________________________________________________________

Name ______________________________ Date ______________ Class ______________

CHAPTER 6

BUILDING YOUR PORTFOLIO CHECKLIST

# LEARNING

## *Building Your Portfolio*

**STEP 1 (CHAPTER 6)**

Select a specific subject area, such as math, writing, foreign languages, or a general subject that interests you. Formulate a plan to help parents and educators teach this subject to elementary school children in the most effective manner.

Include answers to the following questions in your plan: How can the principles of classical conditioning, operant conditioning, and observational learning be applied to specific learning situations? Is the PQ4R method more effective in some areas than in others?

Create visual materials to help you formulate this part of your plan. Create a rough draft of this part of your report, and show it to your teacher. Use the following checklist.

______ State the specific subject area that interests you.

______ Formulate a plan to help parents and educators teach the subject to elementary school children.

______ Explain how you can apply the principles of classical conditioning, operant conditioning, and observational learning to the specific learning situations in your plan.

______ Explain whether the PQ4R method is more effective in some areas than in others.

______ Create visual materials to help you formulate this part of your plan.

______ Create a rough draft of this part of your plan.

______ Teacher's initials

CHAPTER

# 7



# MEMORY

## *Improving Memory*

**BACKGROUND INFORMATION** Chapter 7 presents students with information about memory. The chapter describes what psychologists have learned about memory. Students are given an overview of the three threes of memory: the three kinds, the three processes, and the three stages. The chapter also presents information about forgetting and ways to improve memory. In this assessment activity, students are asked to use this information to create a bulletin board display explaining some tips for improving memory.

**PURPOSE** To create a bulletin board display that explains some tips for improving memory.

**TEACHING STRATEGIES** Before students begin work on the bulletin board display, discuss with them the strategies that can be implemented to improve memory. List the strategies on the board, and have students give examples of each strategy.

Before students begin the assignment, have them examine the Display or Exhibit Assessment form on page 27 to review the standards by which they will be evaluated.

Provide students with bulletin board space throughout the school—in the library, cafeteria, hallways, classrooms, and so on. Allow time for students to assemble their bulletin board displays.

After students have completed their bulletin board displays, have them evaluate their work by using the Display or Exhibit Assessment form on page 27. Use the same form for your evaluation of the work.

**TIME ESTIMATE** Approximately 3 50-minute class sessions, or about 2 1/2 hours.

CHAPTER 7

PORTFOLIO: TASK SHEET

# MEMORY

## *Improving Memory*

**INTRODUCTION**
Psychologists have performed numerous experiments and other studies about memory and forgetting. As a result of these experiments and studies, they have identified various strategies that people can use to help improve their memory. Knowing and understanding these strategies can help students retain information and improve their study habits.

**TASK** Create a bulletin board display showing strategies to help students improve memory.

**TARGET AUDIENCE** Your bulletin board display should target students in your school.

**PURPOSE** The purpose of the bulletin board display is to provide your target audience with strategies that will help them improve their memory. The bulletin board display should suggest several strategies for improving memory and give examples to help explain the suggestions.

**PROCEDURE**

1. Choose several strategies psychologists have identified that people can use to improve their memory.
2. Decide on the kinds of examples you want to use to help explain and illustrate the strategies that you chose.
3. Create a rough draft of your bulletin board display. Be sure to include a title or heading and several strategies and examples of how to use the strategies.
4. Edit the first draft of your bulletin board display.
5. Rewrite the draft, and use the Display or Exhibit Assessment form to identify improvements that you can make.
6. Assemble your bulletin board display.

**ASSESSMENT**
Use the Display or Exhibit Assessment form to evaluate your bulletin board display.

Name ______________________________ Date ______________ Class ______________

CHAPTER

7

PORTFOLIO: ASSESSMENT

# MEMORY

## *Display or Exhibit Assessment*

This form is designed to help you evaluate your display or exhibit. Your teacher will use the same form to evaluate your work. Read the criteria listed. Then circle the number to the right of each criterion that most closely reflects your personal evaluation of your display or exhibit.

| Criteria | Performance Levels<br>Excellent | <br>Average | <br>Unsatisfactory |
|---|---|---|---|
| 1. The theme of the display or exhibit is clear. | 3 | 2 | 1 |
| 2. The physical objects (if used) are appropriate for the display or exhibit, and they are well organized. | 3 | 2 | 1 |
| 3. The graphics (such as words, symbols, colors, patterns, and designs) help carry out the theme and add interest to the display or exhibit. | 3 | 2 | 1 |
| 4. The design is effective and catches the attention of its intended audience. | 3 | 2 | 1 |
| 5. The information presented in the display or exhibit is accurate and conveys the most important points relating to the theme. | 3 | 2 | 1 |
| 6. The display or exhibit is neat and visually appealing. | 3 | 2 | 1 |
| 7. The display or exhibit is creative and communicates its intended message. | 3 | 2 | 1 |

To compute the score for your display or exhibit, add the numbers you have circled and divide the result by 7.

▶ **Total score for display or exhibit** ______________

The display or exhibit can be improved by ______________________________

______________________________________________

______________________________________________

Name ______________________________ Date ______________ Class ______________

CHAPTER 7

BUILDING YOUR PORTFOLIO CHECKLIST

# MEMORY

## *Building Your Portfolio*

**STEP 2 (CHAPTER 7)**

Continue to formulate a plan that would help parents and educators teach the subject you have chosen to elementary school children in the most effective manner. Include answers to the following questions in your plan: How can children be taught to improve their memory? How can they minimize the various types of forgetting?

Create visual materials to help you formulate this part of your plan. Create a rough draft of this part of your report, and show it to your teacher. Use the following checklist.

______ Determine a way in which children can be taught to improve their memory for learning the subject.

______ Determine a way in which children can minimize the various types of forgetting when learning the subject.

______ Create visual materials to help you formulate this part of your plan.

______ Create a rough draft of this part of your plan.

______ Teacher's initials

CHAPTER

# 8 THINKING AND LANGUAGE



## *Solving Problems*

**BACKGROUND INFORMATION** Chapter 8 presents students with information about thinking and language. The chapter discusses various thinking processes, such as problem solving, reasoning, and decision making. Students are given an overview of the relationship between thinking and language. In this assessment activity, students are asked to use this information to give an oral presentation with visual aids to explain the ABCDEs of problem solving.

**PURPOSE** To give an oral presentation with visual aids that explains the ABCDEs of problem solving.

**TEACHING STRATEGIES** Before students begin work on the oral presentation with visual aids, ask them to review the steps involved in solving the problems described in Figure 8.1. Ask students to explain how these problems were solved using the ABCDEs of problem solving.

Before students begin the assignment, have them examine the Oral Presentation with Visual Aids Assessment form on page 31 to review the standards by which they will be evaluated.

If possible, videotape students as they practice their oral presentations with visual aids. Allow students to view themselves on the videotapes to see how they can improve their oral presentations.

After students have completed their oral presentations, have them evaluate their work by using the Oral Presentation with Visual Aids Assessment form on page 31. Use the same form for your evaluation of their work.

**TIME ESTIMATE** Approximately 4 50-minute class sessions, or about 3 1/2 hours.

Name ______________________ Date ____________ Class ____________

CHAPTER 8

PORTFOLIO: TASK SHEET

# THINKING AND LANGUAGE

## *Solving Problems*

**INTRODUCTION**

There are many approaches to problem solving. Some psychologists who have studied various approaches to problem solving believe that the best way to solve a problem is to use the ABCDEs. The ABCDEs include assessing the problem, brainstorming approaches, choosing an approach, doing the problem, and evaluating the results. Knowing how to use the ABCDEs of problem solving can be a helpful lifelong tool.

**TASK** Give an oral presentation with visual aids to explain how to apply the ABCDEs of problem solving.

**TARGET AUDIENCE** Your oral presentation with visual aids should target students in your school.

**PURPOSE** The purpose of the oral presentation with visual aids is to provide your target audience with a concrete example of using the ABCDEs of problem solving.

**PROCEDURE**

1. Think of problems that you or someone you know have encountered. Choose one of the problems to show how the ABCDEs of problem solving can be applied to the problem.
2. Decide on the visual aids in your presentation. The visual aids should help clarify the information in your oral presentation.
3. Write an outline for your oral presentation.
4. Create a rough draft of your oral presentation. Be sure to include an opening statement that explains the purpose of your oral presentation, a body of information that provides details, and a summary that ties the information together. In your rough draft, indicate when and how you will use the visual aids in your presentation.
5. Edit the first draft of your oral presentation with visual aids.
6. Practice the oral presentation with visual aids in front of a video camera or in front of a mirror. Watch your presentation. Make appropriate adjustments to your delivery. Listen to your presentation. Make changes in your presentation based on your observations.
7. Rework the draft of your oral presentation. Make sure that your visual aids add to the clarity of the presentation. Use the Oral Presentation with Visual Aids Assessment form to identify improvements that you can make.
8. Using index cards, write short notes that will help you remember what you want to say in your oral presentation. Indicate on the note cards when and how to use visual aids.
9. Practice the final draft of your oral presentation with visual aids.
10. Deliver your oral presentation with visual aids to your audience.

**ASSESSMENT**

Use the Oral Presentation with Visual Aids Assessment form to evaluate your oral presentation.

Name ______________________________ Date ______________ Class ______________

CHAPTER 8

PORTFOLIO: ASSESSMENT

# THINKING AND LANGUAGE

## *Oral Presentation with Visual Aids Assessment*

This form is designed to help you evaluate your oral presentation with visual aids. Your teacher will use the same form to evaluate your work. Read the criteria listed. Then circle the number to the right of each criterion that most closely reflects your personal evaluation of your oral presentation with visual aids.

| | Performance Levels | | |
|---|---|---|---|
| **Criteria** | **Excellent** | **Average** | **Unsatisfactory** |
| 1. The purpose of the oral presentation with visual aids is clear. | 3 | 2 | 1 |
| 2. The presentation is well organized and easy to follow. | 3 | 2 | 1 |
| 3. The information in the oral presentation with visual aids is accurate and relevant to the theme. The details and examples presented make the main ideas meaningful to the audience. | 3 | 2 | 1 |
| 4. The presenter can be seen and heard by everyone in the audience. | 3 | 2 | 1 |
| 5. The presenter speaks fluently and uses notes sparingly. | 3 | 2 | 1 |
| 6. The presenter makes eye contact with the audience. | 3 | 2 | 1 |
| 7. The oral presentation with visual aids is interesting and holds the attention of the audience. | 3 | 2 | 1 |
| 8. The visual aids add to the clarity of the presentation. | 3 | 2 | 1 |
| 9. The use of the visual aids is effective. | 3 | 2 | 1 |
| 10. The visual aids can be seen by all members of the audience. | 3 | 2 | 1 |
| 11. The presenter is confident and shows interest and enthusiasm. | 3 | 2 | 1 |
| 12. The presenter ties the information together with a closing summary. | 3 | 2 | 1 |

To compute the score for your oral presentation with visual aids, add the numbers you have circled and divide the result by 12.

▶ **Total score for oral presentation with visual aids** ______________

The oral presentation with visual aids can be improved by ______________________

Name ______________________________ Date ______________ Class ______________

CHAPTER 8

BUILDING YOUR PORTFOLIO CHECKLIST

# THINKING AND LANGUAGE

## *Building Your Portfolio*

**STEP 3 (CHAPTER 8)**

Continue to formulate a plan that would help parents and educators teach the subject you have chosen to elementary school children in the most effective manner. Include answers to the following questions in your plan: How do most children learn to solve problems, reason, make decisions, and use language? Are those methods effective? Why or why not? How could they be improved?

Create visual materials to help you formulate this part of your plan. Create a rough draft of this part of your report, and show it to your teacher. Use the following checklist.

______ Explain how most children solve problems, reason, make decisions, and use language in the subject area.

______ Explain whether or not those methods of problem solving, reasoning, decision making, and using language are effective.

______ Determine a way to improve the methods of problem solving, reasoning, decision making, and using language.

______ Create visual materials to help you communicate this part of your plan.

______ Create a rough draft of this part of your plan.

______ Teacher's initials

# INTELLIGENCE

## *Influencing Intelligence*

**BACKGROUND INFORMATION** Chapter 9 presents information about intelligence. The chapter examines how intelligence is defined and measured. Students learn about group differences in intelligence and about factors that influence intelligence. In this assessment activity, students are asked to use this information to write a newspaper article that uses the results of psychological studies of intelligence to explain to parents how they can influence the intelligence of their children in positive ways.

**PURPOSE** To write a newspaper article that informs parents of ways that they can influence the intelligence of their children positively.

**TEACHING STRATEGIES** Before students begin work on the newspaper article, ask them to compare and contrast the theories and studies about intelligence by the following psychologists: Spearman, Thurstone, Gardner, Sternberg, Goleman, Rauscher, Shaw, and Ky. Ask students to formulate generalizations about intelligence based on these theories and studies. Write these generalizations on the board. Explain to students that they might use the generalizations in their newspaper article. Remind students that generalizations they make in their newspaper articles should be supported with information from psychological theories or studies.

Before students begin the assignment, have them examine the Newspaper Article Assessment form on page 35 to review the standards by which they will be evaluated.

Have students write the newspaper article to certain specifications such as column width—2 inches, 40 lines per column, 3 columns. Have students use a computer to type their newspaper article if possible.

Encourage students to include a photograph and caption with their article. Arrange to have the newspaper articles published in the school newspaper or in the local community's newspaper.

After students have completed their newspaper articles, have them evaluate their work by using the Newspaper Article Assessment form on page 35. Use the same form for your evaluation of the work.

**TIME ESTIMATE** Approximately 5 50-minute class sessions, or about 4 hours.

Name ______________________________ Date ______________ Class ______________

CHAPTER 9

PORTFOLIO: TASK SHEET

# INTELLIGENCE

## *Influencing Intelligence*

**INTRODUCTION**

Although there are many unanswered questions about intelligence, psychologists have formed theories about what makes up intelligence. They have also conducted studies about intelligence that have identified certain factors that influence intelligence. Some factors, such as heredity, cannot change intelligence. It is important, however, that parents realize that environmental factors can and do affect intelligence. By knowing and understanding the environmental factors that influence intelligence, parents have a better opportunity to influence their children's intelligence in positive ways.

**TASK** Write a newspaper article that explains how parents can influence the intelligence of their children in positive ways.

**TARGET AUDIENCE** Your newspaper article should target parents of young children.

**PURPOSE** The purpose of the newspaper article is to provide your target audience with strategies for improving or enhancing their children's intelligence. The newspaper article should include the results of studies about environmental influences on intelligence. The article should give examples of ways in which parents can influence their childrens' intelligence.

**PROCEDURE**

1. Research psychological studies of environmental influences on intelligence. Take notes on information you want to include in your newspaper article.
2. Make an outline of the information you want to include in your newspaper article.
3. Create a rough draft of your newspaper article, including a headline.
4. Edit the rough draft of your newspaper article, and use the Newspaper Article Assessment form to identify improvements you can make.
5. Select a photo or picture from a magazine and write a caption for it to use in your newspaper article.
6. Write a final copy of your article, and present it to your teacher.

**ASSESSMENT**

Use the Newspaper Article Assessment form to evaluate your newspaper article.

Name ______________________________ Date ______________ Class ______________

CHAPTER 9

PORTFOLIO: ASSESSMENT

# INTELLIGENCE

## *Newspaper Article Assessment*

This form is designed to help you evaluate your newspaper article. Your teacher will use the same form to evaluate your work. Read the criteria listed. Then circle the number to the right of each criterion that most closely reflects your personal evaluation of your newspaper article.

| | Performance Levels | | |
|---|---|---|---|
| **Criteria** | **Excellent** | **Average** | **Unsatisfactory** |
| 1. The main topic of the newspaper article is clearly stated in the first paragraph. | 3 | 2 | 1 |
| 2. The newspaper article is well organized. The most important facts are near the beginning. The supporting details follow. A final paragraph ties the article together. | 3 | 2 | 1 |
| 3. The information in the newspaper article is correct. | 3 | 2 | 1 |
| 4. The style of the newspaper article is straightforward and factual. | 3 | 2 | 1 |
| 5. The newspaper article reflects correct spelling, grammar, and punctuation. | 3 | 2 | 1 |
| 6. The headline is a good summary of the main thrust of the newspaper article. | 3 | 2 | 1 |
| 7. The quotations are accurate and support the article but do not make up most of the article. | 3 | 2 | 1 |
| 8. Sources of quotations are included in the article. | 3 | 2 | 1 |
| 9. The photo or picture and caption support the text of the newspaper article. | 3 | 2 | 1 |

To compute the score for your newspaper article, add the numbers you have circled and divide the result by 9.

▶ **Total score for newspaper article** ______________

The newspaper article can be improved by ______________________________

______________________________________________________________

______________________________________________________________

Name ______________________________ Date ______________ Class ______________

CHAPTER

9

BUILDING YOUR PORTFOLIO CHECKLIST

# INTELLIGENCE

## *Building Your Portfolio*

**STEP 4 (CHAPTER 9)**

Complete the plan that would help parents and educators teach the subject you have chosen to elementary school children in the most effective manner. Include answers to the following question in your plan: What can parents and educators do to help the development of each child's intelligence?

Create visual materials to help you formulate this part of your plan. Create a rough draft of this part of your report, and show it to your teacher. Organize the written and visual materials you have completed for this unit and complete the final draft of your report. Use the following checklist.

______ State the specific subject area that interests you.

______ Formulate a plan to help parents and educators teach the subject to elementary school children.

______ Explain what parents can do to help the development of their child's intelligence.

______ Explain what educators can do to enhance the development of each child's intelligence.

______ Create visual materials to help you formulate this part of your plan.

______ Create a rough draft of this part of your plan.

______ Organize the written and visual materials you have completed for this unit.

______ Complete the final draft of your report.

______ Teacher's initials

CHAPTER

# 10



# INFANCY AND CHILDHOOD

## *Understanding Child Development*

**BACKGROUND INFORMATION** Chapter 10 presents information about infant and child development. The chapter explains the major theories of development. Students are given an overview of the physical, social, and cognitive development of infants and children. In this assessment activity, students are asked to use this information to create a graphic presentation of their data.

**PURPOSE** To create a graphic presentation of data based on psychological studies of infant and child development.

**TEACHING STRATEGIES** Before students begin work on the graphic presentation of data, ask them to review the graphic presentation of data shown in Figures 10.1, 10.2, 10.3, and 10.4 in Chapter 10. Ask students to describe the kinds of graphics used to show information. *(graph, diagram, charts)* Remind students that graphics are used to show information at a glance—a way to easily interpret and compare data. Have students find other examples of graphic presentation of data in their textbook. Discuss with students when it is appropriate to use each type of graphic.

Before students begin the assignment, have them examine the Graphic Presentation of Data Assessment form on page 39 to review the standards by which they will be evaluated.

After students have completed their graphic presentations of data, have them evaluate their work by using the Graphic Presentation of Data Assessment form on page 39. Use the same form for your evaluation of the work.

**TIME ESTIMATE** Approximately 4 50-minute class sessions, or about 3 1/2 hours.

Name ______________________ Date ____________ Class ____________

CHAPTER 10

PORTFOLIO: TASK SHEET

# INFANCY AND CHILDHOOD

## *Understanding Child Development*

**INTRODUCTION**
Psychologists study human development of people of all ages. The results of these studies are used for many purposes. For example, the results of psychological studies of infants have been used to teach new parents how to properly care for their newborns. The results of psychological studies of children have been used to help parents and educators know the best age at which children can learn certain skills. What are some other possible uses of the results of child development studies?

**TASK** Create a graphic presentation of data about human development in infancy and childhood.

**TARGET AUDIENCE** Your graphic presentation of data should target developers of infant and childhood clothes and toys.

**PURPOSE** The purpose of the graphic presentation of data is to provide your target audience with information to help them understand the stages of physical, social, and cognitive development in infants and children. The graphic presentation of data will help the developers of infant and childhood clothes and toys make informed decisions about the sizes and kinds of clothes to make and the kinds of toys to make. The graphic presentation of data will be presented in the form of charts, graphs, and diagrams.

**PROCEDURE**

1. Review the results of psychological studies of infant and childhood development described in Chapter 10. Take notes on information you want to include in your graphic presentation of data. Your presentation should include information about the following: physical development, social development, and cognitive development.
2. Note the information you want to include in your graphic presentation of data.
3. Create a rough draft of your graphic presentation of data. Be sure to include appropriate titles.
4. Edit the rough draft of your graphic presentation of data.
5. Rework the rough draft, and use the Graphic Presentation of Data Assessment form to identify improvements you can make.
6. Make a final copy of your graphic presentation of data, and give it to your teacher.

**ASSESSMENT**
Use the Graphic Presentation of Data Assessment form to evaluate your graphic presentation of data.

Name ______________________ Date ____________ Class ____________

CHAPTER 10

PORTFOLIO: ASSESSMENT

# INFANCY AND CHILDHOOD

## *Graphic Presentation of Data Assessment*

This form is designed to help you evaluate your graphic presentation of data. Your teacher will use the same form to evaluate your work. Read the criteria listed. Then circle the number to the right of each criterion that most closely reflects your personal evaluation of your graphic presentation of data.

| | Performance Levels | | |
|---|---|---|---|
| **Criteria** | **Excellent** | **Average** | **Unsatisfactory** |
| 1. The main theme of the graphic presentation of data is clear. | 3 | 2 | 1 |
| 2. The graphics are well organized. | 3 | 2 | 1 |
| 3. The information in the graphics is correct. | 3 | 2 | 1 |
| 4. The graphics follow the proper formats. | 3 | 2 | 1 |
| 5. The graphics reflect correct spelling, grammar, and punctuation. | 3 | 2 | 1 |
| 6. The titles of the graphics summarize the information given. | 3 | 2 | 1 |
| 7. The graphics are skillfully executed and contribute to the visual impact. | 3 | 2 | 1 |
| 8. The graphics effectively communicate the necessary information to the intended audience. | 3 | 2 | 1 |

To compute the score for your graphic presentation of data, add the numbers you have circled and divide the result by 8.

▶ **Total score for graphic presentation of data** ____________

The graphic presentation of data can be improved by ______________________

______________________________________________

______________________________________________

Name ______________________________ Date ______________ Class ______________

CHAPTER 10

BUILDING YOUR PORTFOLIO CHECKLIST

# INFANCY AND CHILDHOOD

## *Building Your Portfolio*

**STEP 1 (CHAPTER 10)**

Select a culture other than that of the United States. Research the culture to find out how human development in this culture differs from human development in the United States. Write a research report that describes some differences in human development between the culture you chose and that of the United States. Include answers to the following questions in your report: Are there any physical developmental differences between infants and young children in the culture you researched and those in the United States? If so, what might account for them?

Create a rough draft of the first part of your report, and show it to your teacher. Use the following checklist.

______ State the culture you chose to research.

______ Determine whether there are any physical developmental differences between infants and young children in the culture you researched and those in the United States.

______ Explain the physical developmental differences between infants and young children in the culture you researched and those in the United States.

______ Explain what might account for the differences in physical development between infants and young children in the culture you researched and those in the United States.

______ Create a rough draft of the first part of your research report.

______ Teacher's initials

CHAPTER

# 11

PORTFOLIO: TEACHER'S NOTES

# ADOLESCENCE

## *Analyzing Issues of Adolescence*

**BACKGROUND INFORMATION** Chapter 11 presents students with information about physical changes that occur during adolescence and the psychological effects of these changes. Chapter 11 describes adolescent social development and explains identity formation. Students are given an overview of the kinds of challenges that adolescents face in today's society.

**PURPOSE** To conduct a survey that asks teens to respond to questions that address the major topics of adolescent development.

**TEACHING STRATEGIES** Before students begin work on the survey, review with them the major topics teens face—physical and psychological development, social development, identity formation, and other challenges of adolescence. Ask students to identify a topic and questions they would ask other teens about adolescent development. Write some of the questions on the board. Discuss with students the questions you think would be appropriate to include in a survey about adolescent development. Explain why some questions might be inappropriate to include in a survey (privacy issue).

Discuss with students possible formats that they could use to present questions in a survey. Will the survey have respondents answer by circling an answer, writing an essay, or doing something else? How can they organize the data collected?

Before students begin the assignment, have them examine the Survey Assessment form on page 43 to review the standards by which they will be evaluated.

Tell students that respondents should not be asked to sign their names to the surveys. Confidentiality must be respected. Ask students to keep the survey to a reasonable length—respondents should be able to complete the survey in 10 to 15 minutes.

After students have completed their surveys, have them evaluate their work by using the Survey Assessment form on page 43. Use the same form for your evaluation of the work.

**TIME ESTIMATE** Approximately 4 50-minute class sessions, or about 3 1/2 hours.

Name ______________________ Date ____________ Class ____________

CHAPTER

# 11

PORTFOLIO: TASK SHEET

# ADOLESCENCE

## *Analyzing Issues of Adolescence*

### INTRODUCTION

High school students experience changes throughout their adolescence. Among the changes are physical growth, social development, and the formation of an identity. Teens also face many challenges. These changes and challenges can make adolescence a confusing and stressful time. Knowing that other teens face similar changes and challenges and knowing how they cope with those changes and challenges can help teens understand the changes they are experiencing.

**TASK** Formulate and conduct a survey that addresses a major topic of adolescent development.

**TARGET AUDIENCE** Your survey should target students in your school.

**PURPOSE** The purpose of the survey is to gather information about how teens cope with the changes and challenges of adolescence.

### PROCEDURE

1. Choose a major topic about adolescent development.
2. Make an outline of the main points you want to cover in your survey.
3. Create a rough draft of the survey.
4. Edit the first draft of your survey. Use the Survey Assessment form on page 43 to identify improvements that you can make.
5. Revise your survey.
6. Make a final draft of your survey.
7. Create a plan for conducting the survey.
8. Conduct the survey.
9. Organize the responses of the survey into a summary or a graphic organizer.
10. Present your survey and its findings to your target audience.

### ASSESSMENT

Use the Survey Assessment form to evaluate your survey.

Name ______________________ Date ____________ Class ____________

CHAPTER 11

PORTFOLIO: ASSESSMENT

# ADOLESCENCE

## *Survey Assessment*

This form is designed to help you evaluate your survey. Your teacher will use the same form to evaluate your work. Read the criteria listed. Then circle the number to the right of each criterion that most closely reflects your personal evaluation of the survey.

| Criteria | Performance Levels<br>Excellent | <br>Average | <br>Unsatisfactory |
|---|---|---|---|
| 1. The topic of the survey is clear. | 3 | 2 | 1 |
| 2. The survey is well organized. | 3 | 2 | 1 |
| 3. The questions in the survey are written clearly and are relevant to the topic. | 3 | 2 | 1 |
| 4. The population chosen to be surveyed is well suited to the topic. | 3 | 2 | 1 |
| 5. The plan for administering the survey ensures validity and reliability. | 3 | 2 | 1 |
| 6. The data from the survey are organized, labeled, and complete enough for one to draw conclusions. | 3 | 2 | 1 |
| 7. The survey shows that the student understands the purpose of the assignment. | 3 | 2 | 1 |
| 8. The student has written an appropriate summary of the responses or has constructed an appropriate graphic showing the responses. | 3 | 2 | 1 |

To compute the score for your survey, add the numbers you have circled and divide the result by 8.

▶ **Total score for survey** ____________

The survey can be improved by ______________________________

______________________________

______________________________

Name ______________________________ Date ______________ Class ______________

CHAPTER

# 11

BUILDING YOUR PORTFOLIO CHECKLIST

# ADOLESCENCE

## *Building Your Portfolio*

**STEP 2 (CHAPTER 11)**

Continue researching information about some differences in human development between the culture you chose and that of the United States. Include answers to the following questions in your report: How long does childhood last in this culture? What is considered an appropriate age for children to start working, if at all? How long does adolescence last in this culture? Do you think James Marcia's categories of adolescent identity status apply in this culture? Why or why not?

Create a rough draft for this part of your report, and show it to your teacher. Use the following checklist.

______ Determine how long childhood lasts in the culture you researched.

______ Explain the difference between the length of childhood in the culture you researched and the length of childhood in the United States.

______ Determine whether there is an appropriate age for children to start working in the culture you researched.

______ Explain whether there is a difference between the appropriate age for children to start working in the culture you researched and in the United States.

______ Determine how long adolescence lasts in the culture you researched.

______ Compare the length of adolescence in the culture you researched with the length of adolescence in the United States.

______ Determine whether James Marcia's categories of adolescent identity status apply to the culture you researched. Explain why they do or do not apply.

______ Create a rough draft of this part of your research report.

______ Teacher's initials

CHAPTER

# 12



# ADULTHOOD

## *Illustrating Stages of Adulthood*

**BACKGROUND INFORMATION** Chapter 12 presents students with information about adulthood. The chapter describes the three broad stages of adulthood: young adulthood, middle adulthood, and late adulthood. The text provides an overview of the key developmental tasks of adults in each of the three broad stages. In this assessment activity, students are asked to use this information to create a photo essay showing the key developmental tasks of each of the three broad stages of the adult years.

**PURPOSE** To create a photo essay that illustrates the key developmental tasks of the three broad stages of adulthood.

**TEACHING STRATEGIES** Before students begin work on the photo essay, review with them text Figures 12.1, 12.2, and 12.5. Discuss with students the kinds of developmental tasks that have been listed for young adulthood, middle adulthood, and late adulthood. Ask students to list additional developmental tasks for each stage of adulthood.

Before students begin the assignment, have them examine the Photo Essay Assessment form on page 47 to review the standards by which they will be evaluated.

After students have completed their photo essays, have them evaluate their work by using the Photo Essay Assessment form on page 47. Use the same form for your evaluation of the work.

Arrange to have the photo essays displayed in the school library. Along with the photo essays, ask the school librarian to display books about the developmental stages ofadulthood, such as those written by the authors quoted in Chapter 12.

**TIME ESTIMATE** Approximately 5 50-minute class sessions, or about 4 hours.

Name ______________________ Date ____________ Class ____________

CHAPTER

# 12

PORTFOLIO: TASK SHEET

# ADULTHOOD

## *Illustrating Stages of Adulthood*

### INTRODUCTION

Many myths have been applied to the three stages of adulthood. As adolescents interact with adults and approach adulthood themselves, it is important for them to know and understand the realities of adulthood. Knowing the key developmental tasks of each stage of adulthood can help adolescents better understand the adults with whom they interact. Knowing and understanding the key developmental tasks of each stage of adulthood can also help adolescents maintain a positive attitude about their own aging process.

**TASK** Create a photo essay that uses photographs and captions to illustrate and describe the key developmental tasks of the three broad stages of adulthood: young adulthood, middle adulthood, and late adulthood.

**TARGET AUDIENCE** Your photo essay should target adolescents in your school and other visitors to the library.

**PURPOSE** The purpose of the photo essay is to provide your target audience with realistic illustrations and captions of the key development tasks of the three stages of adulthood: young adulthood, middle adulthood, and late adulthood.

### PROCEDURE

1. Decide on the format of your photo essay—album, bulletin board display, poster, and so on.
2. Create sections in your photo essay that address young adulthood, middle adulthood, and late adulthood.
3. Choose the key developmental tasks for each stage of adulthood that you want to illustrate in your photo essay.
4. Select photos for the key developmental tasks that you chose. You might find photos in family albums or in magazines and newspapers. You can also take photographs yourself.
5. Create a rough draft of your photo essay. Decide how to arrange the photographs, and write the caption that will accompany each photograph.
6. Edit the first draft of your photo essay.
7. Rework the draft of your photo essay, and use the Photo Essay Assessment form to identify improvements that you can make.
8. Make a final copy of your photo essay, and present it to your teacher.

### ASSESSMENT

Use the Photo Essay Assessment form to evaluate your photo essay.

Name ______________________________ Date ______________ Class ______________

CHAPTER 12

PORTFOLIO: ASSESSMENT

# ADULTHOOD

## *Photo Essay Assessment*

This form is designed to help you evaluate your photo essay. Your teacher will use the same form to evaluate your work. Read the criteria listed. Then circle the number to the right of each criterion that most closely reflects your personal evaluation of the photo essay.

| | Performance Levels | | |
|---|---|---|---|
| **Criteria** | **Excellent** | **Average** | **Unsatisfactory** |
| 1. The theme and purpose of the photo essay are clear. | 3 | 2 | 1 |
| 2. The photo essay is well organized. | 3 | 2 | 1 |
| 3. The photo essay demonstrates an understanding of the purpose of the assignment. | 3 | 2 | 1 |
| 4. The photographs and the captions are appropriate and convey the important points connected to the theme. | 3 | 2 | 1 |
| 5. The arrangement of the photographs is attractive and flows smoothly through the essay. | 3 | 2 | 1 |
| 6. The photo essay is neat and legible. | 3 | 2 | 1 |
| 7. The photo essay contains the required elements. | 3 | 2 | 1 |

To compute the score for your photo essay, add the numbers you have circled and divide the result by 7.

▶ **Total score for photo essay** ______________

The photo essay can be improved by ________________________________________

______________________________________________________________________

______________________________________________________________________

Name ______________________________ Date ______________ Class ______________

CHAPTER

# 12

BUILDING YOUR PORTFOLIO CHECKLIST

# ADULTHOOD

## *Building Your Portfolio*

**STEP 3 (CHAPTER 12)**

Continue researching information about some differences in human development between the culture you chose and that of the United States. Include answers to the following questions in your report: At what age are members of this culture considered adults? Does the age differ for boys and girls? Are the developmental tasks of young adulthood in this culture comparable to Erikson's list on text page 276? What is the average age for marriage in this culture? Does it differ greatly from that in the United States? If so, what might account for the difference? What are the culture's attitudes toward aging and the elderly?

Create a rough draft of this part of your report, and show it to your teacher. Write a final draft of the report, incorporating information from this chapter and from Chapters 10 and 11. Use the following checklist.

______ Determine at what age members of the culture you researched are considered adults and whether the age differs for boys and girls. Compare these ages with the age that boys and girls are considered adults in the United States.

______ Compare and contrast the developmental tasks of young adulthood in the culture you researched with Erikson's list on page 276 of your textbook.

______ Determine the average age for marriage in the culture you researched. Decide whether the average age for marriage in the culture you researched differs greatly from that in the United States. If it does, explain possible reasons for the difference.

______ Explain whether there is a difference between the attitudes toward aging and the elderly in the culture you researched and those in the United States.

______ Create a rough draft of this part of your research report.

______ Write a final draft of the research report, incorporating the information from Chapters 10, 11, and 12.

CHAPTER 13



# MOTIVATION AND EMOTION

## *Understanding Motivation and Emotion*

**BACKGROUND INFORMATION** Chapter 13 discusses the theories of motivation and emotion. The chapter describes the effects that biological needs, psychological needs, and emotions have on human behavior. The text provides an overview of the factors that affect motivation. In this assessment activity, students are asked to use this information to create a theater presentation that examines how emotions lead us to behave in certain ways.

**PURPOSE** To create a theater presentation that examines the ways in which emotions lead us to behave in certain ways.

**TEACHING STRATEGIES** Before students begin work on the theater presentation, discuss with them plays they have seen in which motivation and emotion are themes, such as *Hamlet,* or other plays by Shakespeare they may have studied. Ask students to describe the motivation and emotion that led the characters in the plays to behave in certain ways. Discuss with students which theories of motivation and theories of emotion might apply to the characters in each play.

Before students begin the assignment, have them examine the Theater Presentation Assessment form on page 51 to review the standards by which they will be evaluated.

Encourage students to keep their theater presentations to no more than 10 to 20 minutes.

Arrange to have the theater presentations videotaped and made available to users of the school library. Along with the videotapes of the theater presentations, ask the school librarian to display other plays with themes about motivation and emotion, such as *Death of a Salesman, Hamlet,* and *Les Miserables.*

When students have completed their theater presentations, have them evaluate their work by using the Theater Presentation Assessment form on page 51. Use the same form for your evaluation of the work.

**TIME ESTIMATE** Approximately 10 50-minute class sessions, or about 8 to 9 hours.

Name ______________________ Date __________ Class __________

CHAPTER 13

PORTFOLIO: TASK SHEET

# MOTIVATION AND EMOTION

## *Understanding Motivation and Emotion*

### INTRODUCTION

Why do we do the things we do? Psychologists agree that motivation and emotion cause people to behave in certain ways. Psychologists, however, do not always agree about the nature of motivation and emotion. There are several theories that explain the nature of motivation and emotion. Understanding these theories helps explain the reasons for human behavior. Knowing the possible reasons for certain behavior can help you better understand yourself and others.

**TASK** Create a theater presentation that examines the reasons why people behave in certain ways.

**TARGET AUDIENCE** Your theater presentation should target students and others who use the school library.

**PURPOSE** The purpose of the theater presentation is to provide your target audience with explanations of why people behave in certain ways.

### PROCEDURE

1. Decide on motives and emotions that you want to include in your theater presentation. Use these motives and emotions to explain the behavior of your characters.
2. Create a rough draft of your script for the theater presentation. Decide how many acts will be in your presentation.
3. Edit the first draft of your script for the theater presentation.
4. Rehearse the script for the theater presentation.
5. Rework the draft of your script for the theater presentation on the basis of suggestions you may have as a result of the rehearsal. Also use the Theater Presentation Assessment form to identify improvements that you can make.
6. Make a final copy of your script.
7. Decide on the kinds of visuals, props, and costumes you want for the theater presentation.
8. Hold a dress rehearsal for the theater presentation using the final script.
9. Videotape and/or give a live performance of your theater presentation.

### ASSESSMENT

Use the Theater Presentation Assessment form to evaluate your theater presentation.

Name ______________________ Date __________ Class __________

CHAPTER 13

PORTFOLIO: ASSESSMENT

# MOTIVATION AND EMOTION

## *Theater Presentation Assessment*

This form is designed to help you evaluate your theater presentation. Your teacher will use the same form to evaluate your work. Read the criteria listed. Then circle the number to the right of each criterion that most closely reflects your personal evaluation of the theater presentation.

| | Performance Levels | | |
|---|---|---|---|
| **Criteria** | **Excellent** | **Average** | **Unsatisfactory** |
| 1. The theme and purpose of the theater presentation are clear. | 3 | 2 | 1 |
| 2. The actor(s) can be heard and understood by the audience. | 3 | 2 | 1 |
| 3. The dialogue is appropriate, interesting, and pertinent to the topic. | 3 | 2 | 1 |
| 4. The character(s) is (are) appropriate to the theme and purpose. | 3 | 2 | 1 |
| 5. The information presented in the theater presentation is accurate and relevant to the topic. | 3 | 2 | 1 |
| 6. The theater presentation effectively communicates its message to the audience. | 3 | 2 | 1 |
| 7. The visuals, props, and costumes add to the clarity and effectiveness of the theater presentation. | 3 | 2 | 1 |

To compute the score for your theater presentation, add the numbers you have circled and divide the result by 7.

▶ **Total score for theater presentation** __________

The theater presentation can be improved by ______________________

______________________

______________________

Name ______________________________ Date ______________ Class ______________

CHAPTER

# 13

BUILDING YOUR PORTFOLIO CHECKLIST

# MOTIVATION AND EMOTION

## *Building Your Portfolio*

**STEP 1 (CHAPTER 13)**

Select a public setting (for example, a playground, a park, or a fast-food restaurant) in which you can observe the behavior of children and their parents. Choose two individual children for two case studies and take notes on their actions. Write a report on the behavior observed in your case studies. Include answers to the following questions in your report after you have reviewed Maslow's hierarchy of needs on text page 302: What physiological and/or safety needs did the child exhibit? (For instance, was the child acting tired?) What love and belongingness and/or esteem needs did the child exhibit? (For example, was the child clinging to his or her parent?)

Create a rough draft of the first part of your report, and show it to your teacher. Use the following checklist.

______ Describe the public setting you selected to observe the behavior of two children.

______ State the sexes of the children and parents and the approximate ages of the children.

______ Using Maslow's hierarchy of needs on page 302 in your textbook, determine the physiological and/or safety needs exhibited by each child.

______ Using Maslow's hierarchy of needs, determine the love and belongingness and/or esteem needs exhibited by each child.

______ Create a rough draft of the first part of your research report.

______ Teacher's initials

CHAPTER

# 14



# THEORIES OF PERSONALITY

## *Describing Personality*

**BACKGROUND INFORMATION** Chapter 14 discusses theories of personality. The chapter describes personality characteristics and explains how personality develops. Students are given an overview of five approaches to the study of personality. In this assessment activity, students are asked to use this information to write a story to explain a theory of personality development.

**PURPOSE** To write a story that applies a theory of personality development to a fictional character.

**TEACHING STRATEGIES** Before students begin work on the story, read them some excerpts from the novel *Walden Two* by B. F. Skinner. Discuss with students how Skinner created this story to explain the psychological concept of behaviorism. Next have students reread the metaphor about the seaweed withstanding the pounding surf (by Carl Rogers) on page 336 in the textbook. Ask students to explain how Rogers used this metaphor to explain the psychological concept of humanism.

Before students begin the assignment, have them examine the Story Presentation of Psychology Concept Assessment form on page 55 to review the standards by which they will be evaluated.

When students have completed their story presentations, have them evaluate their work by using the Story Presentation of Psychology Concept Assessment form on page 55. Use the same form for your evaluation of the work.

Arrange to have the stories available in the school library. Along with the stories written by students, ask the school librarian to display other books with fictional presentations of psychology concepts.

**TIME ESTIMATE** Approximately 7 50-minute class sessions, or about 6 hours.

Name ______________________________ Date ______________ Class ______________

CHAPTER 14

PORTFOLIO: TASK SHEET

# THEORIES OF PERSONALITY

## *Describing Personality*

**INTRODUCTION**
What does it mean when someone talks about having a "personality conflict" with someone else? What do you mean when you describe someone as having a "great personality"? Psychologists define *personality* as the pattern of feelings, motives, and behaviors that sets one person apart from others. Psychologists study personality development so that they can predict how people will react in various life situations. There are several theories to explain how personality affects behavior. Understanding these theories can help you better understand yourself and others.

**TASK** Create a story presentation that explains one or more of the following theories of personality development: trait, psychoanalytic, learning, humanistic, and sociocultural.

**TARGET AUDIENCE** Your story presentation should target students in your school.

**PURPOSE** The purpose of the story presentation is to use one or more of the personality theories to explain why the main characters in the story behave as they do.

**PROCEDURE**

1. Review the five theories of personality development described in Chapter 14.
2. Decide on one or more theories of personality to include in your story. Use the theory or theories to explain the behavior of the main characters in your story.
3. Brainstorm ideas that you might want to include in your story.
4. Create a rough draft of your story.
5. Edit the first draft of your story. Use the Story Presentation of Psychology Concept Assessment form to identify improvements that you can make.
6. Make a final copy of your story, and present it to your teacher.

**ASSESSMENT**
Use the Story Presentation of Psychology Concept Assessment form to evaluate your story presentation.

Name ______________________________ Date ______________ Class ______________

CHAPTER 14

PORTFOLIO: ASSESSMENT

# THEORIES OF PERSONALITY

## *Story Presentation of Psychology Concept Assessment*

This form is designed to help you evaluate your story presentation. Your teacher will use the same form to evaluate your work. Read the criteria listed. Then circle the number to the right of each criterion that most closely reflects your personal evaluation of the story presentation.

| Criteria | Performance Levels<br>Excellent | <br>Average | <br>Unsatisfactory |
|---|---|---|---|
| 1. The theme of the story is appropriate for the writing assignment. | 3 | 2 | 1 |
| 2. Information from the textbook is applied to the story. | 3 | 2 | 1 |
| 3. The character(s) is (are) appropriate to the theme and purpose. | 3 | 2 | 1 |
| 4. The ideas in the story flow smoothly. | 3 | 2 | 1 |
| 5. The story reflects correct spelling, punctuation, and grammar. | 3 | 2 | 1 |
| 6. The story has a clear beginning, middle, and end. | 3 | 2 | 1 |
| 7. The story effectively communicates its intended message to the audience. | 3 | 2 | 1 |
| 8. The writing is neat, legible, and clear. | 3 | 2 | 1 |

To compute the score for your story presentation, add the numbers you have circled and divide the result by 8.

▶ **Total score for story presentation** ______________

The story presentation can be improved by ______________________________

______________________________

______________________________

Name ______________________ Date ____________ Class ____________

CHAPTER 14

BUILDING YOUR PORTFOLIO CHECKLIST

# THEORIES OF PERSONALITY

## *Building Your Portfolio*

**STEP 2 (CHAPTER 14)**

Continue working on your report about the behavior observed in your case studies. Include answers to the following questions in your report: What personality traits did the child exhibit? According to Freud's theory, what developmental stage is the child in? What stage, according to Erikson? How would a behaviorist view the child's behavior? How would a humanist?

Create a rough draft of this part of your report, and show it to your teacher. Use the following checklist.

______ Describe the personality traits exhibited by each child.

______ Determine the developmental stage of each child according to Freud's theory and according to Erikson's theory.

______ Explain how a behaviorist would view each child's behavior.

______ Explain how a humanist would view each child's behavior.

______ Create a rough draft of this part of your research report.

______ Teacher's initials

CHAPTER



# 15 PSYCHOLOGICAL TESTS

## *Improving Test Performance*

**BACKGROUND INFORMATION** Chapter 15 discusses psychological tests. The chapter explains the purposes and characteristics of psychological tests. Students are given an overview of the kinds of psychological tests available and strategies for taking tests and avoiding test anxiety. In this assessment activity, students are asked to use this information to create a graphic presentation of data that will help other students realize that there are things they can do to help improve their test performance.

**PURPOSE** To create a graphic presentation of data that compares scores on tests students take before and after they are given tips on taking tests.

**TEACHING STRATEGIES** Before students begin work on the graphic presentation of data, have them review the general tips on taking tests. Then have students make a list of kinds of test items, such as multiple-choice questions and true or false questions. Ask students to discuss some tips for taking tests for each specific kind of test item.

Encourage students to research sources other than their textbooks to find tips for improving test performance.

Before students begin the assignment, have them examine the Graphic Presentation of Data Assessment form on page 59 to review the standards by which they will be evaluated.

If possible, show students samples of infographics in newspapers and magazines. Encourage students to add visuals such as infographics to their graphic presentations of data to help make their graphic presentations interesting and easy to understand. Remind students that the information shown in an infographic must be factual as well as creative and eye-catching.

After students have completed their graphic presentations of data, have them evaluate their work by using the Graphic Presentation of Data Assessment form on page 59. Use the same form for your evaluation of the work.

**TIME ESTIMATE** Approximately 8 50-minute class sessions, or about 6 to 7 hours.

Name ______________________ Date ____________ Class ____________

CHAPTER

# 15

PORTFOLIO: TASK SHEET

# PSYCHOLOGICAL TESTS

## *Improving Test Performance*

### INTRODUCTION

Does it seem like every time you turn around you are being tested for one thing or another? Your perceptions may not be too far off. There are tests that assess potential for learning, abilities, attitudes, feelings, behaviors, and interests. You cannot study for these kinds of tests. The tests you take in your classroom, however, are mostly achievement tests. You know that studying for those tests can improve your test performance. It is also possible to improve test performance by learning tips for taking tests.

**TASK** Create a graphic presentation of data that compares scores on tests students take before and after learning tips for taking tests.

**TARGET AUDIENCE** Your graphic presentation of data should target people who take achievement tests.

**PURPOSE** The purpose of the graphic presentation of data is to provide your target audience with information to help them determine whether or not people can improve their test results by learning tips for taking tests.

### PROCEDURE

1. Review the tips for taking tests in Chapter 15.
2. Make arrangements with a teacher to administer a test to several classes. If possible, the tests should have two similar forms, such as Form A and Form B. Review the two forms of the test for kinds of test items.
3. Make a list of tips for taking tests based on the kinds of items given on the test forms, as well as other helpful hints that might apply. Practice explaining the tips for taking tests to family members.
4. Administer Form A of the test to the students in each class. When the students have finished, collect the tests.
5. Explain the tips for taking tests to the students. Then administer Form B of the test. When the students have finished, collect the tests.
6. Correct Form A and Form B of the tests.
7. Decide on the types of graphics you want to use in your presentation to show the results of the tests.
8. Make a rough draft of your graphic presentation of data, including titles.
9. Edit the rough draft of your graphic presentation of data.
10. Rework the rough draft, and use the Graphic Presentation of Data Assessment form to identify improvements you can make.
11. Make a final copy of your graphic presentation, and give it to your teacher.

### ASSESSMENT

Use the Graphic Presentation of Data Assessment form to evaluate your graphic presentation of data.

Name ______________________ Date __________ Class __________

CHAPTER 15

PORTFOLIO: ASSESSMENT

# PSYCHOLOGICAL TESTS

## *Graphic Presentation of Data Assessment*

This form is designed to help you evaluate your graphic presentation of data. Your teacher will use the same form to evaluate your work. Read the criteria listed. Then circle the number to the right of each criterion that most closely reflects your personal evaluation of your graphic presentation of data.

| | Performance Levels | | |
|---|---|---|---|
| **Criteria** | **Excellent** | **Average** | **Unsatisfactory** |
| 1. The main subject of the graphic presentation of data is clear. | 3 | 2 | 1 |
| 2. The graphics are well organized. | 3 | 2 | 1 |
| 3. The information in the graphics is accurate. | 3 | 2 | 1 |
| 4. The graphics follow the proper formats. | 3 | 2 | 1 |
| 5. The graphics reflect correct spelling, grammar, and punctuation. | 3 | 2 | 1 |
| 6. The titles of the graphics summarize the information given. | 3 | 2 | 1 |
| 7. The graphics are skillfully executed and contribute to the visual impact. | 3 | 2 | 1 |
| 8. The graphics are effective in communicating necessary information to the intended audience. | 3 | 2 | 1 |

To compute the score for your graphic presentation of data, add the numbers you have circled and divide the result by 8.

▶ **Total score for graphic presentation of data** __________

The graphic presentation of data can be improved by ______________________

______________________________________________

______________________________________________

Name ______________________ Date ____________ Class ____________

CHAPTER

# 15

BUILDING YOUR PORTFOLIO CHECKLIST

# PSYCHOLOGICAL TESTS

## *Building Your Portfolio*

**STEP 3 (CHAPTER 15)**

Continue working on your report about the behavior observed in your case studies. Include answers to the following questions in your report: Did the child attempt to explore his or her environment or seek stimulation? What emotions did the child exhibit? What facial expressions or body language did you use as clues to the child's emotional state?

Create a rough draft of this part of your report, and show it to your teacher. Use the following checklist.

______ Explain whether or not each child attempted to explore his or her environment or seek stimulation.

______ Describe the emotions exhibited by each child.

______ Describe the facial expressions or body language that you used as clues to each child's emotional state.

______ Create a rough draft of this part of your research report.

______ Teacher's initials

CHAPTER

# 16



# GENDER ROLES

## *Describing Gender Roles*

**BACKGROUND INFORMATION** Chapter 16 discusses gender and gender roles. The chapter describes gender differences in cognitive abilities, personality, and behavior. The text provides an overview of gender typing, how and when it develops in people, how gender roles have changed over time, and how gender roles vary from culture to culture. In this assessment activity, students are asked to create a survey to administer to middle-aged and older adults about changes in gender roles over the last 50 years.

**PURPOSE** To conduct interviews with middle-aged and older adults to learn how gender roles have changed over the last 50 years.

**TEACHING STRATEGIES** Before students begin work on the survey, have them work in small groups to review the material in the chapter. Using the information in the chapter, each group should brainstorm questions to ask middle-aged and older adults about how gender roles have changed over time. Have one person in each group record the questions. When the groups have finished, ask the recorders to read their groups' questions. Write them on the chalkboard. Discuss with students whether the questions are appropriate for such an interview. Then have students select appropriate questions from the chalkboard to use.

Encourage students to interview three or four people. Students should interview both males and females.

Stress to students that although they will have a standard list of questions to use in the interview, they may want to modify them slightly on the basis of the responses from the interviewees. Students should try to direct the interview back to the standard questions.

Before students begin the assignment, have them examine the Interview Assessment form on page 63 to review the standards by which they will be evaluated.

After students have completed their interviews, have them evaluate their work by using the Interview Assessment form on page 63. Use the same form for your evaluation of the work.

**TIME ESTIMATE** Approximately 7 50-minute class sessions, or about 6 hours.

Name ______________________ Date ____________ Class ____________

CHAPTER

# 16 GENDER ROLES

PORTFOLIO: TASK SHEET

## *Describing Gender Roles*

### INTRODUCTION

All cultures have certain expectations about the behavior of males and females. You have learned that gender roles in this country have changed over time. In what way have gender roles changed? Have these changes been positive or negative? What, if any, new gender stereotypes exist in the United States today?

**TASK** Conduct interviews with middle-aged and older adults to learn how they think gender roles have changed over the last 50 years. Present your findings in a final report.

**TARGET AUDIENCE** The target audience for your interview findings should be your classmates.

**PURPOSE** The purpose of the interviews is to provide your target audience with information that describes how gender roles in the United States have changed over time.

### PROCEDURE

1. From the list of appropriate questions that groups have brainstormed, select the questions for your interviews.
2. Edit the questions, using the Interview Assessment form to help you.
3. Make a final draft of the interview questions.
4. Make a plan to conduct your interviews. You can conduct the interviews face-to-face or over the telephone. Consider videotaping or tape-recording your interviews. Be sure to obtain permission from the interviewees.
5. Conduct your interviews. Remember to modify your interview questions on the basis of the responses of the interviewees.
6. Organize the information from your interviews into a final report.
7. Present the final report to your teacher.

### ASSESSMENT

Use the Interview Assessment form to evaluate your interviews.

Name ______________________ Date ____________ Class ____________

CHAPTER 16

PORTFOLIO: ASSESSMENT

# GENDER ROLES

## *Interview Assessment*

This form is designed to help you evaluate your interviews. Your teacher will use the same form to evaluate your work. Read the criteria listed. Then circle the number to the right of each criterion that most closely reflects your personal evaluation of the interview.

| | Performance Levels | | |
|---|---|---|---|
| **Criteria** | **Excellent** | **Average** | **Unsatisfactory** |
| 1. The main topic of the interviews is clear. | 3 | 2 | 1 |
| 2. The interview questions are relevant to the main topic of the interviews. | 3 | 2 | 1 |
| 3. The interview questions are well organized and flow smoothly through the interviews. | 3 | 2 | 1 |
| 4. The interview questions show that the student understands the purpose of the assignment. | 3 | 2 | 1 |
| 5. The findings of the interviews as presented in the final report are relevant to the topic. | 3 | 2 | 1 |
| 6. Proper spelling, grammar, and punctuation are used in the final report on the findings of the interviews. | 3 | 2 | 1 |

To compute the score for your interviews, add the numbers you have circled and divide the result by 6.

▶ **Total score for interviews** ____________

The interviews can be improved by ______________________________

______________________________

______________________________

Name ______________________ Date ____________ Class ____________

CHAPTER 16

BUILDING YOUR PORTFOLIO CHECKLIST

# GENDER ROLES

## *Building Your Portfolio*

**STEP 4 (CHAPTER 16)**

Continue working on the report about the behavior observed in your case studies. Include answers to the following questions in your report: Did the child exhibit any behavior that is stereotypical of his or her sex? Did the parent (or parents) say or do anything to reinforce behavior that is "appropriate" for the child's sex?

Create a rough draft of this part of your report, and show it to your teacher. Write a final draft of the research report, incorporating the information and observations from this chapter and Chapters 13, 14, and 15. Use the following checklist.

______ Explain whether or not each child exhibited any behavior that is stereotypical of his or her sex.

______ Explain whether or not each parent (or parents) said or did anything to reinforce behavior that is "appropriate" for the child's sex.

______ Create a rough draft of this part of your research report.

______ Write a final draft of the research report, incorporating information and observations from Chapters 13, 14, 15, and 16.

______ Teacher's initials

CHAPTER 17

# STRESS AND HEALTH

## *Coping with Stress*

**BACKGROUND INFORMATION** Chapter 17 presents students with information about the relationship between stress and health. The chapter describes the causes of stress and the body's response to stress. Students are given an overview of how stress affects a person's health. In this assessment activity, students are asked to use this information to write a research report about ways to cope with stress.

**PURPOSE** To write a research report that suggests effective ways of coping with stress.

**TEACHING STRATEGIES** Before students begin work on the research report, have them review the studies about stress that are referred to in Chapter 17. Point out that many studies have been conducted to find ways to relieve stress. Encourage students to use the studies discussed in Chapter 17 as starting points in their search for information for their research report.

Have students review the graphics in Chapter 17. Instruct students to include graphics in their reports to illustrate and support the information presented. Remind students of the importance of including sources for their information.

Before students begin the assignment, have them examine the Research Report Assessment form on page 67 to review the standards by which they will be evaluated.

After students have completed their research reports, have them evaluate their work by using the Research Report Assessment form on page 67. Use the same form for your evaluation of the work.

**TIME ESTIMATE** Approximately 7 50-minute class sessions, or about 6 hours.

Name ______________________________ Date ______________ Class ______________

CHAPTER 17

PORTFOLIO: TASK SHEET

# STRESS AND HEALTH

## *Coping with Stress*

### INTRODUCTION

At one time or another, everyone experiences stress. How a person deals with the stress makes a difference in that person's overall health. What are some helpful ways to cope with stress? What is the most effective coping strategy for you to relieve stress?

**TASK** Write a research report that suggests effective ways of coping with stress.

**TARGET AUDIENCE** Your research report should target people who are looking for methods for coping with stress.

**PURPOSE** The purpose of the research report is to provide your target audience with evidence that convinces them to try one or more of your suggested methods for coping with stress.

### PROCEDURE

1. Decide which coping method you want to include in your research report.
2. Research three methods. Take notes on information you want to include in your report. Write the notes on index cards. Include your sources on the cards.
3. Using your research notes, make an outline for your research report.
4. Using your research notes and outline, create a rough draft of your research report. Include graphics to support the information in the report.
5. Edit the rough draft of your report.
6. Rewrite the draft, and use the Research Report Assessment form to identify improvements that you can make.
7. Make a final copy of your research report, and present it to your teacher.

### ASSESSMENT

Use the Research Report Assessment form to evaluate your research report.

Name ______________________________ Date ______________ Class ______________

CHAPTER

17

PORTFOLIO: ASSESSMENT

# STRESS AND HEALTH

## *Research Report Assessment*

This form is designed to help you evaluate your research report. Your teacher will use the same form to evaluate your work. Read the criteria listed. Then circle the number to the right of each criterion that most closely reflects your personal evaluation of the research report.

| | Performance Levels | | |
|---|---|---|---|
| **Criteria** | **Excellent** | **Average** | **Unsatisfactory** |
| 1. The topic of the research report is clear. | 3 | 2 | 1 |
| 2. The research report is well organized into paragraphs with clear main ideas and appropriate supporting details. | 3 | 2 | 1 |
| 3. The conclusion summarizes the main points of the report. | 3 | 2 | 1 |
| 4. The research report demonstrates that the purpose of the assignment is understood. | 3 | 2 | 1 |
| 5. The research report includes the student's own ideas. | 3 | 2 | 1 |
| 6. Appropriate sources are included in the research report. | 3 | 2 | 1 |
| 7. The graphics add to the clarity of information in the research report. | 3 | 2 | 1 |
| 8. The research report reflects correct spelling, grammar, and punctuation. | 3 | 2 | 1 |
| 9. The research report is neat and legible. | 3 | 2 | 1 |

To compute the score for your research report, add the numbers you have circled and divide the result by 9.

▶ **Total score for research report** ______________

The research report can be improved by ______________________________

______________________________________________

______________________________________________

Name ______________________________ Date ______________ Class ______________

CHAPTER

# 17

BUILDING YOUR PORTFOLIO CHECKLIST

# STRESS AND HEALTH

## *Building Your Portfolio*

**STEP 1 (CHAPTER 17)**
Review the symptoms of psychological disorders covered in the unit. Then read the fictional case histories that depict individuals with psychological problems or disorders. Identify and list the symptoms of the individual in each case.

Create a rough draft for the first part of your chart, and show it to your teacher. Use the following checklist.

______ Identify the key symptoms of each patient.

______ List the key symptoms of each patient to include in your chart.

______ Make a rough draft of the part of the chart titled Key Symptoms.

______ Teacher's initials

CHAPTER

# 18



# PSYCHOLOGICAL DISORDERS

## *Identifying Psychological Disorders*

**BACKGROUND INFORMATION** Chapter 18 presents students with information about the types of psychological disorders. The chapter describes the effects of psychological disorders on the people with the disorders and on their family and friends. The text provides an overview of the theories that help explain the psychological disorders. In this assessment activity, students are asked to use this information to write a story that illustrates a psychological disorder.

**PURPOSE** To write a story in which the main character exhibits a psychological disorder.

**TEACHING STRATEGIES** Before students begin work on the story, have them review the psychological disorders described in Chapter 18. Ask them to identify stories in which a character has one of the psychological disorders described in Chapter 18. Have students describe the physical signs and symptoms used in the story to describe the psychological disorder.

Read students an excerpt from Judith Rapoport's book *The Boy Who Couldn't Stop Washing*. Discuss with students the descriptions Rapoport uses to explain the psychological disorder of the main character in her book.

Before students begin the assignment, have them examine the Story Presentation of Psychological Concept Assessment form on page 71 to review the standards by which they will be evaluated.

After students have completed their stories, have them evaluate their work by using the Story Presentation of Psychological Concept Assessment form on page 71. Use the same form for your evaluation of the work.

**TIME ESTIMATE** Approximately 6 50-minute class sessions, or about 5 hours.

Name ______________________ Date ____________ Class ____________

CHAPTER 18

PORTFOLIO: TASK SHEET

# PSYCHOLOGICAL DISORDERS

## *Identifying Psychological Disorders*

**INTRODUCTION**
Psychological disorders affect not only the people with the disorders but also their family and friends. Identifying the signs and symptoms of psychological disorders can, however, help ease the distress that often accompanies such disorders. People with psychological disorders can seek professional help to identify and treat the disorders. Therefore, it is important to know the signs and symptoms of psychological disorders.

**TASK** Write a story that describes the signs and symptoms of one or more psychological disorders.

**TARGET AUDIENCE** Your story should target students in your school.

**PURPOSE** The purpose of the story is to provide your target audience with information about the behavior associated with one or more psychological disorders. The story should use that information to describe and explain the actions of the main characters.

**PROCEDURE**

1. Review the psychological disorders described in Chapter 18.
2. Decide on the psychological disorders that your story will focus on. Use the information about the psychological disorders to explain the behavior of the main characters in the story. Your story should include descriptions of the effect of the disorders on the main characters and on his or her (their) relationships with family and friends.
3. Make a list of ideas to include in your story.
4. Create a rough draft of your story.
5. Edit the rough draft of your story. Use the Story Presentation of Psychological Concept Assessment form to identify improvements that you can make.
6. Make a final copy of your story, and present it to your teacher.

**ASSESSMENT**
Use the Story Presentation of Psychological Concept Assessment form to evaluate your story.

Name ______________________ Date ____________ Class ____________

CHAPTER 18

PORTFOLIO: ASSESSMENT

# PSYCHOLOGICAL DISORDERS

## *Story Presentation of Psychological Concept Assessment*

This form is designed to help you evaluate your story. Your teacher will use the same form to evaluate your work. Read the criteria listed. Then circle the number to the right of each criterion that most closely reflects your personal evaluation of your story.

| Criteria | Performance Levels Excellent | Average | Unsatisfactory |
|---|---|---|---|
| 1. The theme of the story is appropriate for the writing assignment. | 3 | 2 | 1 |
| 2. Information from the textbook is applied to the story. | 3 | 2 | 1 |
| 3. The writing is neat, legible, and clear. | 3 | 2 | 1 |
| 4. The character(s) in the story is (are) appropriate to the theme and purpose. | 3 | 2 | 1 |
| 5. The ideas in the story flow smoothly. | 3 | 2 | 1 |
| 6. The story reflects correct spelling, punctuation, and grammar. | 3 | 2 | 1 |
| 7. The story has a clear beginning, middle, and end. | 3 | 2 | 1 |
| 8. The story effectively communicates its intended message to the audience. | 3 | 2 | 1 |

To compute the score for your story presentation, add the numbers you have circled and divide the result by 8.

▶ **Total score for story presentation** ____________

The story presentation can be improved by ______________________________

______________________________________________

______________________________________________

Name ______________________________ Date ______________ Class ______________

CHAPTER 18

BUILDING YOUR PORTFOLIO CHECKLIST

# PSYCHOLOGICAL DISORDERS

## *Building Your Portfolio*

**STEP 2 (CHAPTER 18)**

Review the symptoms of psychological disorders covered in the unit. Reread the fictional case histories that depict individuals with psychological problems or disorders. Think of a possible diagnosis or diagnoses for each case. Keep in mind that more than one diagnosis may be possible or that further information may be needed to narrow the possibilities.

Create a rough draft of this part of your chart, and show it to your teacher. Use the following checklist.

______ Identify a probable diagnosis or diagnoses for the patient in each case study.

______ Describe any further information you may need to better diagnose each individual's problem or disorder.

______ Create a rough draft of the parts of the chart titled Probable Diagnosis or Diagnoses and Further Information Needed to Diagnose or Treat the Disorder.

______ Teacher's initials

CHAPTER

# 19



# METHODS OF THERAPY

## *Explaining Methods of Therapy*

**BACKGROUND INFORMATION** Chapter 19 discusses the methods of therapy for types of psychological disorders. The chapter describes the goals and techniques of psychoanalysis, humanistic therapy, cognitive therapy, behavior therapy, and biological therapy. The text provides an overview of the pros and cons of each type of therapy. In this assessment activity, students are asked to use this information to write an advice column in a newspaper to explain the methods of therapy applied to psychological disorders.

**PURPOSE** To write a newspaper advice column that informs people about the methods of therapy used to help people with psychological disorders.

**TEACHING STRATEGIES** Before students begin the advice columns, provide them with the following example of a scenario and questions:

My wife has insomnia. As a result of this condition, she cannot keep a job. Whom should she see for help? What kind of therapy is used for this problem? Are there support groups for people with insomnia? Is it possible that she can get better?

Then ask each student to pretend that she or he is writing to a newspaper columnist who gives advice about health concerns. Students should provide imaginary scenarios in which a person describes a psychological problem or disorder that they or someone they know has. (Students should use the disorders discussed in Chapter 18.) Students should also provide four questions about the therapy for the disorder.

Collect scenarios and questions and edit them. Students will use the edited scenarios and questions as the basis for their advice columns.

Before students begin the assignment, have them examine the Newspaper Advice Column Assessment form on page 75 to review the standards by which they will be evaluated.

After students have completed their newspaper advice columns, have them evaluate their work by using the Newspaper Advice Column Assessment form on page 75. Use the same form for your evaluation of the work.

**TIME ESTIMATE** Approximately 3 50-minute class sessions, or about 2 1/2 hours.

Name ______________________ Date ____________ Class ____________

CHAPTER 19

PORTFOLIO: TASK SHEET

# METHODS OF THERAPY

## *Explaining Methods of Therapy*

### INTRODUCTION

Statistics indicate that 23 percent of the people in the United States experience some kind of psychological disorder in their lifetime. It is likely, therefore, that someone you know will be affected by a psychological disorder. Learning about the various methods of therapy may help the affected person seek appropriate treatment.

**TASK** Write a newspaper advice column that answers questions about the kind of therapy recommended for a specific psychological disorder.

**TARGET AUDIENCE** Your advice column should target your classmates and newspaper readers.

**PURPOSE** The purpose of the advice column is to provide your target audience with answers to questions about therapy for a particular psychological disorder. The advice column should be set up in a question-and-answer format.

### PROCEDURE

1. Submit scenario and questions to the teacher for review.
2. Revise scenario and questions on the basis of the teacher's comments.
3. Use the information in Chapter 19 or in other psychology sources to find the answers to the questions about therapy for the specified psychological disorder.
4. Create a rough draft of your advice column. Include a headline.
5. Edit the rough draft of your advice column. Use the Newspaper Advice Column Assessment form to identify improvements that you can make.
6. Make a final copy of your advice column, and present it to your teacher.

### ASSESSMENT

Use the Newspaper Advice Column Assessment form to evaluate your advice column.

Name ______________________ Date ____________ Class ____________

CHAPTER 19

PORTFOLIO: ASSESSMENT

# METHODS OF THERAPY

## *Newspaper Advice Column Assessment*

This form is designed to help you evaluate your newspaper advice column. Your teacher will use the same form to evaluate your work. Read the criteria listed. Then circle the number to the right of each criterion that most closely reflects your personal evaluation of the advice column.

| | Performance Levels | | |
|---|---|---|---|
| **Criteria** | **Excellent** | **Average** | **Unsatisfactory** |
| 1. The main topic of the advice column is clear. | 3 | 2 | 1 |
| 2. The advice column is well organized. | 3 | 2 | 1 |
| 3. The information in the advice column is correct. | 3 | 2 | 1 |
| 4. The advice column follows the question-and-answer format. | 3 | 2 | 1 |
| 5. The style of the advice column is straightforward and factual. | 3 | 2 | 1 |
| 6. The advice column reflects correct spelling, grammar, and punctuation. | 3 | 2 | 1 |
| 7. The headline is a good summary of the main thrust of the advice column. | 3 | 2 | 1 |
| 8. Sources are given for any quotations used in the advice column. | 3 | 2 | 1 |

To compute the score for your newspaper advice column, add the numbers you have circled and divide the result by 8.

▶ **Total score for newspaper advice column** ____________

The advice column can be improved by ______________________________

______________________________________________

______________________________________________

Name ______________________________ Date ______________ Class ______________

CHAPTER 19

BUILDING YOUR PORTFOLIO CHECKLIST

# METHODS OF THERAPY

## *Building Your Portfolio*

**STEP 3 (CHAPTER 19)**

Review the symptoms of psychological disorders and the methods of treatment covered in the unit. Then reread the fictional case histories that depict individuals with psychological problems or disorders. Think of an appropriate treatment for the individual in each case history.

Determine whether further information might be needed to better treat each problem or disorder. Recommend a treatment for each patient and provide reasons for your recommendation. Create a rough draft of this part of your chart. Incorporate this part of your chart with the parts you created for Chapters 17 and 18. Show the final draft of the entire chart to your teacher. Use the following checklist.

______ Describe any further information you may need to treat each problem or disorder.

______ Recommend treatment for each patient.

______ Explain the reasons for the recommended treatment.

______ Create a rough draft of the parts of the chart titled Further Information Needed to Diagnose or Treat the Disorder, Recommendation for Treatment, and Reasons for Recommendation.

______ Incorporate the parts of the chart from Chapters 17, 18, and 19, and make a final draft of the entire chart.

______ Teacher's initials

CHAPTER

# 20



# SOCIAL COGNITION

## *Understanding Social Cognition*

**BACKGROUND INFORMATION** Chapter 20 presents students with information about social cognition. The chapter describes how attitudes and other aspects of social cognition affect the ways in which people perceive and act toward others. The text provides an overview of the factors involved in persuasion. In this assessment activity, students are asked to use these factors to give an oral presentation that attempts to persuade their audience.

**PURPOSE** To give an oral presentation that attempts to persuade people to adopt a certain belief.

**TEACHING STRATEGIES** Before students begin working work on the oral presentation, have them watch a television commercial. Tell students to take notes as they analyze the following factors in the commercial: methods of persuasion, the messenger (trustworthiness, physical attractiveness, similarity to audience), the situation, primacy and recency effects, and nonverbal communication. Ask students to share their analyses. Discuss the effectiveness of each commercial on the basis of these factors. Point out to students that the factors they analyzed are things they want to keep in mind when planning their oral presentation.

Before students begin the assignment, have them examine the Oral Presentation Without Visual Aids Assessment form on page 79 to review the standards by which they will be evaluated.

Videotape students as they rehearse their oral presentations. Ask them to analyze their verbal and nonverbal communication and make needed adjustments in their presentations.

After students have completed their oral presentations, have them evaluate their work by using the Oral Presentation Without Visual Aids Assessment form on page 79. Use the same form for your evaluation of the work.

After all oral presentations are completed, hold a class discussion to evaluate the persuasiveness of the presentations.

**TIME ESTIMATE** Approximately 7 50-minute class sessions, or about 6 hours.

Name ______________________ Date ____________ Class ____________

CHAPTER

# 20

PORTFOLIO: TASK SHEET

# SOCIAL COGNITION

## *Understanding Social Cognition*

**INTRODUCTION**

"You need an attitude adjustment." You probably have heard similar statements about "attitude." Attitudes influence many aspects of our lives. How difficult is it to change an attitude? People sometimes change their attitudes when they are persuaded to do so. How persuasive are you?

**TASK** Give an oral presentation without visual aids that argues in favor of something you believe in.

**TARGET AUDIENCE** Your oral presentation should target your classmates.

**PURPOSE** The purpose of the oral presentation is to provide your target audience with a persuasive argument in favor of something you believe in.

**PROCEDURE**

1. Decide on a topic for your oral presentation. The topic should have pros and cons. You should have a strong belief about the topic.
2. Decide on the major issues of your topic. Make a list of the points you want to emphasize in your presentation.
3. Make an outline for your oral presentation.
4. Create a rough draft of your oral presentation. Try to include several methods of persuasion. The oral presentation should include an opening statement that explains the purpose of the presentation, a body of supporting evidence or details, and a summary that ties the information together.
5. Edit the first draft of your oral presentation.
6. Rehearse your oral presentation in front of a mirror or video camera. Analyze the presentation for verbal and nonverbal communication.
7. Rework the presentation on the basis of your analysis of the rehearsal. Also use the Oral Presentation Without Visual Aids Assessment form to identify improvements that you can make.
8. Using index cards, write brief notes that will help you remember what you want to say in your oral presentation.
9. Practice your oral presentation using note cards.
10. Deliver your oral presentation to your audience.

**ASSESSMENT**

Use the Oral Presentation Without Visual Aids Assessment form to evaluate your oral presentation.

Name ______________________ Date ____________ Class ____________

CHAPTER 20

PORTFOLIO: ASSESSMENT

# SOCIAL COGNITION

## *Oral Presentation Without Visual Aids Assessment*

This form is designed to help you evaluate your oral presentation without visual aids. Your teacher will use the same form to evaluate your work. Read the criteria listed. Then circle the number to the right of each criterion that most closely reflects your personal evaluation of your oral presentation without visual aids.

| Criteria | Performance Levels Excellent | Average | Unsatisfactory |
|---|---|---|---|
| 1. The topic and purpose of the oral presentation are clear. | 3 | 2 | 1 |
| 2. The presentation is well organized and easy to follow. | 3 | 2 | 1 |
| 3. The information in the oral presentation is accurate and relevant to the topic. The details and examples presented make the main ideas meaningful to the audience. | 3 | 2 | 1 |
| 4. The presenter speaks fluently without having to constantly read from notes. | 3 | 2 | 1 |
| 5. The presenter makes eye contact with the audience. | 3 | 2 | 1 |
| 6. The oral presentation is interesting and holds the attention of the audience. | 3 | 2 | 1 |
| 7. The presenter appears confident and shows interest and enthusiasm. | 3 | 2 | 1 |
| 8. The presenter ties the information together with a closing summary. | 3 | 2 | 1 |

To compute the score for your oral presentation without visual aids, add the numbers you have circled and divide the result by 8.

▶ **Total score for oral presentation without visual aids** ____________

The oral presentation without visual aids can be improved by ____________

______________________________________

______________________________________

Name ______________________________ Date ______________ Class ______________

CHAPTER

# 20

BUILDING YOUR PORTFOLIO CHECKLIST

# SOCIAL COGNITION

## *Building Your Portfolio*

### STEP 1 (CHAPTER 20)

Choose two TV shows aimed at children—one that is educational and one that is merely entertaining. Watch two or three episodes of each show. Write a report in which you describe the messages in the two shows. Include answers to the following questions in your report: Does the program portray any stereotypes, either positive or negative? Does it depict characters of different cultural and ethnic backgrounds? If so, are these depictions positive or negative? Is the ratio of men to women roughly even? Does the program show characters encountering and dealing with prejudice or discrimination?

Create a rough draft of this part of your report, and show it to your teacher. Use the following checklist.

______ Choose two shows aimed at children—one that is educational and one that is merely entertaining.

______ Watch two or three episodes of each show.

______ Determine whether the programs portray any stereotypes. If so, explain what the stereotypes are and decide whether they are positive or negative.

______ Determine whether the programs depict characters of different cultural and ethnic backgrounds. If so, explain whether the depictions are positive or negative.

______ Note whether the programs have an equal number of male and female characters.

______ Determine whether the programs show characters encountering and dealing with prejudice or discrimination.

______ Create a rough draft of the first part of your report.

______ Teacher's initials

# SOCIAL INTERACTION

## *Identifying Social Groups*

**BACKGROUND INFORMATION** Chapter 21 presents students with information about social interaction. The chapter discusses the factors that attract people to particular groups. It describes polarization—the strengthening of a group's shared attitudes—which occurs as group members discuss and act upon the attitudes they share. The chapter describes how group membership can influence a person's behavior. In this assessment activity, students are asked to create a pamphlet that would help a new student examine the possibilities of school and community groups to join.

**PURPOSE** To create a pamphlet that presents information about school and community clubs, teams, and organizations for teens to join.

**TEACHING STRATEGIES** Before students begin work on the pamphlet, discuss with them the factors to consider when choosing social clubs, teams, and organizations to join. List the factors on the board. Ask students to rank these factors in order of importance. Have students use the most important factors as issues to include in the pamphlets.

Before students begin the assignment, have them examine the Pamphlet Assessment form on page 83 to review the standards by which they will be evaluated.

Before students decide what social clubs, teams, and organizations they want to describe in their pamphlets, have students work in small groups to brainstorm a list of school and community social clubs, teams, and organizations. Students in each group should use the list to help them decide what to include in their pamphlets.

Point out to students that the pamphlets should be visually appealing. Encourage students to review pamphlets for design ideas. Also encourage students to include photographs of the social groups described in the pamphlets.

After students have completed their pamphlets, have them evaluate their work by using the Pamphlet Assessment form on page 83. Use the same form for your evaluation of the work.

**TIME ESTIMATE** Approximately 6 50-minute class sessions, or about 5 hours.

Name ____________________ Date ____________ Class ____________

CHAPTER 21

PORTFOLIO: TASK SHEET

# SOCIAL INTERACTION

## *Identifying Social Groups*

**INTRODUCTION**

Imagine that you and your family have just moved to a new location. How can you meet more people who are your own age? Where can you find groups of people your own age who share your interests?

**TASK** Create a pamphlet that will serve as a guidebook to groups—teams, clubs, and organizations—that teens in your school and community can join.

**TARGET AUDIENCE** Your pamphlet should target new students in your school.

**PURPOSE** The purpose of the pamphlet is to provide your target audience with information about teams, clubs, and organizations in your school and community for teens. The pamphlet should explain the purpose, yearly events, membership qualifications, and meeting dates and times for each team, club, and organization listed.

**PROCEDURE**

1. Do research to find the teams, clubs, and organizations for teens that are available in your school and community.
2. Decide on the teams, clubs, and organizations that you want to include in your pamphlet.
3. Do further research to gather the following information about the teams, clubs, and organizations that will be in your pamphlet: name, purpose or goals, overview of yearly events, membership requirements, dates and times of meetings or events.
4. Create a rough draft of the written information for your pamphlet.
5. Create a design for your pamphlet.
6. Sketch a layout of the information you will present in your pamphlet. Be sure to include space for photographs and other visuals.
7. Edit the first draft of your pamphlet.
8. Rewrite the draft, and use the Pamphlet Assessment form to identify improvements that you can make.
9. Make a final copy of your pamphlet, and give it to your teacher.

**ASSESSMENT**

Use the Pamphlet Assessment form to evaluate your pamphlet.

Name ______________________ Date ____________ Class ____________

CHAPTER 21

PORTFOLIO: ASSESSMENT

# SOCIAL INTERACTION

## *Pamphlet Assessment*

This form is designed to help you evaluate your pamphlet. Your teacher will use the same form to evaluate your work. Read the criteria listed. Then circle the number to the right of each criterion that most closely reflects your personal evaluation of the pamphlet.

| Criteria | Performance Levels<br>Excellent | <br>Average | <br>Unsatisfactory |
|---|---|---|---|
| 1. The purpose of the pamphlet is clear. | 3 | 2 | 1 |
| 2. The pamphlet is well organized. | 3 | 2 | 1 |
| 3. The pamphlet demonstrates knowledge of the purpose of the assignment. | 3 | 2 | 1 |
| 4. The visuals in the pamphlet help clarify the information in the pamphlet. | 3 | 2 | 1 |
| 5. The visuals in the pamphlet are creative and add to the overall look of the pamphlet. | 3 | 2 | 1 |
| 6. The pamphlet is neat and legible. | 3 | 2 | 1 |
| 7. The pamphlet is understandable and interesting. | 3 | 2 | 1 |
| 8. The pamphlet reflects correct spelling, punctuation, and grammar. | 3 | 2 | 1 |
| 9. The pamphlet includes all the required elements. | 3 | 2 | 1 |
| 10. The pamphlet effectively communicates the information to the target audience. | 3 | 2 | 1 |

To compute the score for your pamphlet, add the numbers you have circled and divide the result by 10.

▶ **Total score for pamphlet** ____________

The pamphlet can be improved by ______________________________

______________________________

______________________________

Name ______________________ Date ____________ Class ____________

CHAPTER 21

BUILDING YOUR PORTFOLIO CHECKLIST

# SOCIAL INTERACTION

## *Building Your Portfolio*

**STEP 2 (CHAPTER 21)**

Continue working on the report that describes the messages in the two TV programs you have chosen. Include answers to the following questions in your report: What is the average number of violent occurrences per episode? Is violence or aggression used to address problems routinely, or do characters use other methods to resolve conflicts? In general, is violence glorified, tolerated, or rejected in the program?

Create a rough draft of this part of your report, and show it to your teacher. Write a final draft of the report, incorporating the observations from this chapter and Chapter 20. Use the following checklist.

______ Count the number of violent occurrences per episode of each program.

______ Determine whether violence or aggression is used routinely to address problems. Decide if the characters use other methods to resolve conflicts.

______ Generalize as to whether violence is glorified, tolerated, or rejected in each program.

______ Create a rough draft of this part of your report.

______ Write a final draft of your report, incorporating the observations from Chapters 20 and 21.

______ Teacher's initials